The Book Of Bad Behaviour

For Phoebe—Mercedes Eclair—Powell

and thanks to Richard Allen Turner, Geof Powell and Julie Balloo

First published in Great Britain in 1994 by Virgin Books
an imprint of Virgin Publishing Ltd
332 Ladbroke Grove
London W10 5AH

A catalogue record for this book is available from the British Library

ISBN 0 86269 856 5

Designed by PiNK

Photo credits The Hulton Deutsch Collection pages 5,14,61,62,66,70. Alpha 80. Retna 71.

Printed and bound in Italy by Stiges

THE BOOK OF BAD BEHAVIOUR

Jenny Eclair

Virgin

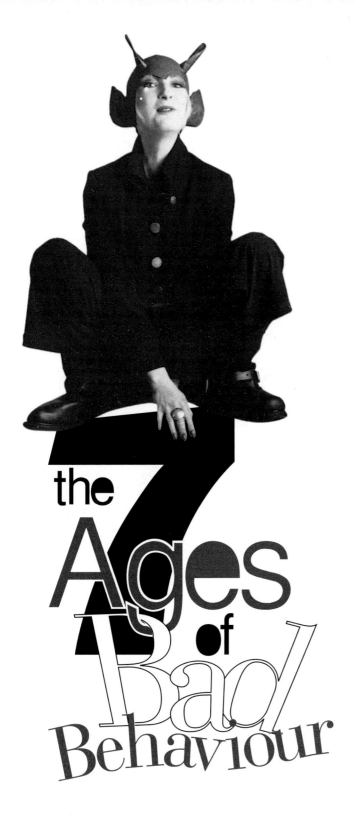

the 7 Ages of Bad Behaviour

BEHAVING BADLY throughout your life requires a great deal of stamina. There's always the temptation to settle down and become a reformed character – TOO depressing. Anyone who feels they want to 'clean up their act' should move to Los Angeles immediately and join all the other boring, born-again, well-behaved people who have fought their demons, given up the booze, the pills and the indiscriminate shagging, and can now wake up without cringing. I wouldn't mind, but these people will try and convert the rest of us, and I hate having things shoved down my throat (know what I mean girls?).

For the rest of us, here are some simple guidelines to behaving badly from pre-cradle to post-grave.

In the beginning

WHEN THE NAUGHTY foetus is ready to be born, he will surprise everybody by flipping into the breech position. The aim is to go for a record-breaking long labour; even funnier if the mother has been attending Natural Childbirth Trust classes and is refusing drugs. These women feel really guilty if, after 40 hours of huffing and puffing and bellowing with pain, they eventually give in and have an epidural. Necessitating a Caesarean is a coup for the naughty foetus, but not as effective as in years gone by when the scars were really massive. These days, Caesarean scars are really neatly tucked under the bikini line, but they still hurt like hell. Personally, I can't see the point in worrying about bikinis after you have given birth: babies ruin your figure for life. If they really wanted to lower the number of teenage pregnancies, they would pay women who've had a couple of kids to visit secondary schools and demonstrate their varicose veins, stretch marks and piles. This would not only put the girls off, but the boys, too.

Every baby looks like Winston Churchill. Reinforce this by smoking big cigars when you're pregnant!

5

BAD BABIES

ARE born looking like the ugliest relative on his side of the family. This will irritate the mother, particularly if she herself was a *Vogue* model, and she will end up spending a fortune on hats to disguise the fact that the child could easily be mistaken for a pig.

Every parent is phobic about its child's development. The bad baby should give them legitimate cause for alarm by refusing to pick up the simplest of skills and, in addition, show all the charisma of suet. In time, the bad baby will learn some tricks; unfortunately, it will not show these off to the health visitor. As soon as a trained professional walks into the room, the bad baby will regress and play stupid: this involves inertia, eye-rolling and failing the seven-month test. This is a simple routine examination: basically, the baby is required to sit up. Despite having achieved this several weeks ago, the bad baby will cross its eyes and slump, dramatically, face down on to the carpet.

Other bad baby tricks include simulating colic, projectile vomiting and mastering the art of having a massive great shit immediately after having been changed and dressed ready to visit grandma. The poo should be evident by the fact that it explodes out around the collar.

The great thing for others about the bad baby is that its parents are so embarrassed about what they have bred that they won't even talk about it, never mind pass round the photos.

HOW TO BEHAVE BADLY WITH ANIMALS

'IT IS IMPORTANT TO KILL ALL YOUR PETS BEFORE YOU GO ON HOLIDAY, BECAUSE YOU CAN'T TRUST ANYONE ELSE TO LOOK AFTER THEM PROPERLY. BETTER SAFE IN THE ARMS OF JESUS THAN NOT HAVING A PROPER WALK EVERY DAY.'

I DO not like animals – I never have. This is because I have a personality disorder. Lots of people, however, are nauseatingly soppy about small furry creatures and will come round to my house and 'get me' after reading this chapter. The only pet I ever owned was a chicken – Juanita. She never left my side, possibly because she was wrapped in cellophane and was squatting in one of those white polystyrene trays.

The most common household pets in this country are cats and dogs. I don't like either. Cats are too superior but at least their poo is small and neat; dogs, on the other hand, do those massive meringue turds bigger than your head. There is so much dog poo where I live that it is impossible to

walk down the street, you just skid. In some respects this is quite useful, because you can get quite a speed up and beat the bus. Old people, however, are always coming a cropper: their balance isn't what it used to be and they're forever crashing into lampposts and smashing their hips.

I can't understand why people throw sticks to dogs. Dogs aren't particularly interested in sticks, what they are interested in is crotches. I don't know why we don't just throw panty liners at them, or bits of old gusset. (I suggest a communal bin of panty things at the entrance of every bit of green space.) If you do decide you want a dog, for protection reasons, it's best to get a very big, dangerous one that you have utterly no control over: cross-breeds are best for erratic and unprovoked acts of viciousness.

I have a girlfriend who owns a very bad dog. We took it to the park one day and it jumped in a duck pond, swam to the other side, clambered on to the bird table, did an enormous Mr Whippy-style shit, got down and swam back, glowing with pride. For a moment, I almost liked it. I also met a Great Dane once, and he had the most enormous testicles I have ever seen. But that's another story entirely and belongs in a

chapter titled 'Stray Backpackers I've Picked Up'.

If you do decide that your life is empty without some dumb animal, use your imagination and get something daft! Get a horse, or perhaps a Vietnamese pot-bellied pig. Or how about a jar of mayonnaise, to which you get ridiculously attached and insist on taking abroad, even though it has to spend months in quarantine?

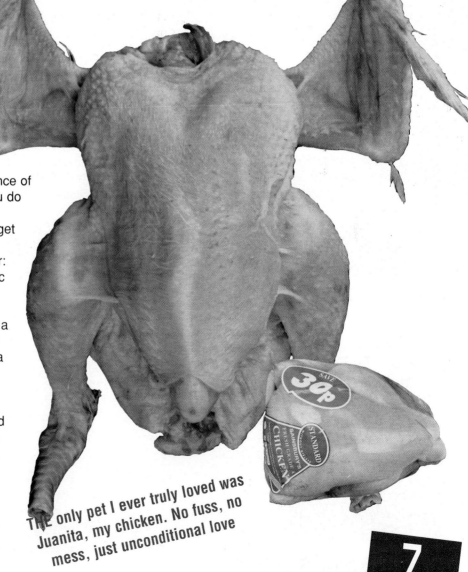

THE only pet I ever truly loved was Juanita, my chicken. No fuss, no mess, just unconditional love

OTHER ANTI-SOCIAL PETS

INCLUDE. . .

HEDGEHOGS

THESE ARE ALWAYS riddled with fleas, keep one in your hankie drawer.

TORTOISES

HAVE YOU EVER seen one crushed on the road? It is a dramatic spectacle and will traumatise any small child.

GOLDFISH (FROM FAIRS)

ALWAYS DIE. To save time and effort, don't even bother to decant them from the plastic bag.

GOLDFISH (BOUGHT FROM PET SHOPS)

ALWAYS DIE and then must be flushed down the toilet, leaving the bowl free for a nice geranium, which will also die and have to be flushed down the toilet.

STICK INSECTS

ARE VERY SCARY and always get out of their box. They have very thin legs which you can accidentally break and then feel very guilty for a long time.

LOCUSTS

STEAM INTO THE contents of your fruit bowl faster than you can say 'plague'.

CHAMELEONS

ARE VERY PESKY critters, they have a habit of disguising themselves to blend in with their environment. I once left one on my dressing table and was half way through cleaning out my ear with what I thought was a cotton bud, when I realised my terrible mistake. It was some time before I regained the power of speech.

SQUIRRELS

MAY LOOK SWEET but they have a nasty habit of killing small children by shinning up trees and raining conkers down on their fragile little skulls.

SNAKES

CAN STRANGLE you in your sleep. They are impossibly faddy with their food and are not happy on a diet of Nestlé's Lucky charms.

TERRAPINS

PEOPLE WILL GIVE you a load of old baloney about how easy terrapins are to keep. Nonsense, give them your bath to live in and they repay your hospitality by taking all the enamel off with their viciously sharp nails.

STAGS

MAKE HOPELESS PETS. You try and give them a cuddle and they get their antlers caught up in your jumper, plucking it really badly.

BULLS

ARE DIFFICULT to bathe and can badly bruise your foot, should they accidentally step on you.

PIGEONS

IT IS NOT A GOOD IDEA to keep pigeons, people will automatically think you're a Northerner, which would never do.

HAMSTERS

FEMALE HAMSTERS are completely unmaternal. I'm not keen on babies, but that's no excuse to eat them, is it? They always start pissing around on the wheel when you're trying to get some kip. Get back at them by blasting daytime TV into their ear-holes. Also, hamsters like to get out of the cage and hide, which means you have to pick up the sofa and see if they're underneath it. As soon as you drop it, you realise you have something else to flush down the toilet.

MOTHS

WOULD BE FINE if they just fluttered prettily around a naked flame as a sort of centre piece at a posh dinner party, but they will insist on chewing cashmere, which means you have to punish them by tugging off their wings and stamping on them.

BADGERS

I HAVE NEVER met a badger with a sense of humour. They are sly and devious and deserve to be turned into shaving brushes.

COCKROACHES

ARE VERMIN, and are, apparently, not a suitable gift for the local kiddies' play group. They are, however, a tasty accompaniment to any Chinese dish. Just chase them around the wok with a little lemongrass.

RATS

WILL TRY AND LULL YOU into a false sense of security by pretending they're really just a sweet, harmless little mouse. You will lavish love and attention on your 'little mouse', until you wake up in the middle of the night with half your face eaten away.

DINGOES

SUFFERED an unfair press back in the Eighties, when they were accused of baby theft and infanticide. In a recent experiment, ten babies were left unsupervised on rocks in the Australian outback. Only three babies were eaten by dingoes. It is therefore fair to say that most dingoes are good with children, but there are a few greedy ones that spoil it for the rest and 'give a dog a bad name'.

WHY WE MUST HARDEN OUR HEARTS AGAINST ANIMALS AND START BEING HORRID TO THEM

MANY LONELY PEOPLE are under the delusion that if they didn't have their dog, they'd be even lonelier. NO. If they didn't have that foul-breathed, farting, leg-shagging, gummy-eyed mongrel that licks its bollocks, then people might want to pop in now and again. There is nothing sadder then hearing someone talking to their cat as if it were a real human being with a brain and a Marks & Spencer's charge card. Listen, cats ladder your tights and so they must die.

AT THE ZOO

THE ONLY POINT in going to a zoo is to watch animals shag. Me, I'd boot out the giant pandas unless they started giving us our money's worth. When I have to be at the zoo, I like to tease the tigers by running around in great big circles, with the wind in my hair, shouting, 'All this space and it's mine. I can go anywhere I like, I may go to Colchester this afternoon.' It's a myth that children like zoos; in my experience they'd rather visit a motorway service station.

ATTAINING THE DYSFUNCTIONAL FAMILY UNIT

IN ORDER TO BEHAVE BADLY at all times, you need to rid yourself of GUILT. It's an entirely worthless emotion, and the one most likely to keep you up all night. Families are the main source of guilt and therefore must be got rid of, either by suffocation or alienation. The trouble with murdering your family is that you might get caught and receive a hefty fine. Plus, killing people is exhausting and you have to remove the evidence. You know what it's like: it's raining, there's a programme you really want to watch on the telly and the last thing you want to do is bundle your nearest and dearest into the boot of your car and spend the night digging shallow graves. Before you know it, they've been hanging round in bin bags for weeks and the neighbours complain about a nasty smell. Far better than giving yourself a criminal record is making them hate you so much that they sever all ties, leaving you free to behave as badly as you like without that dreary sound of your mother crying down the phone every time you get your name in the papers. Alienation might take longer than cutting off their oxygen supply, but it's simpler in the long run.

So, if you've got parents, disown them (unless of course they've got pots of money, in which case emigrate, cause havoc abroad and only come home to collect the dosh when they're dead). Never call them 'Mum' and 'Dad', keep it formal: 'Mr and Mrs Atkinson' will do (even if that's not their name). Sneer at them constantly and roll your eyeballs to the ceiling whenever they dare put forward an opinion. Practice walking out of the room whenever they walk in, and introduce them to your friends as the 'char lady' and 'the gardener'.

The process of eliminating your family from your life can start when you are very young. Small children can cling hysterically to their nursery-school teacher whenever mummy comes to take them home. Infant schools use the 'what I did at the weekend' diary scam in order to pry into the home lives of their pupils. Make sure yours is full of juicy stuff like, 'I spent the weekend being beaten and locked up in a cupboard (even if, in reality, you went to the circus and ate ice-cream), then funny Uncle Matthew with the wobbly leg came round and I sat on his knee and got sweeties for being a good girl.' These revelations will result in you being snatched from your bed in the middle of the night by uniformed officers, which is great, because you'll get tea and biscuits and lots of attention.

Broken homes are a great excuse for behaving badly: being emotionally scarred is brilliant for getting away with things like shoplifting and arson. Confuse your parents until they give up and hand you over to the council. Adopt 'wolf-child' tendencies: scamper around on all fours demanding dog biscuits, reject any offers of bunk beds and insist on sleeping outside in a kennel. You can also bite other children's legs in the playground, and if the dinner lady tells you off, rip her tights with your teeth.

The happy family unit is a fragile thing and is easily shattered – arm yourself with plenty of ammunition and then stand back and watch the cracks appear. Prying and snooping will usually give you all the evidence you need to prove that your parents' relationship is a sham. Go through your mother's drawers and, with any luck, hidden beneath her bras and contraceptive devices there will be a box containing adoption papers regarding an illegitimate child that your father knows nothing about. Bring the subject up at Sunday lunch and remember to stifle any laughter with a sock as it can ruin that golden moment of appalled silence. If this doesn't split your parents up, try harder: the sooner they get divorced, the sooner you can play one off against the other, resulting in bigger, better and more Christmas presents.

Use your mother's paranoia to your advantage: invent a girlfriend for your dad, phone home at every opportunity and hang up when your mother answers. Leave a pair of ladies' knickers in the glove compartment of his car and stuff his pockets with condoms. Another good jape is to ask your dad to pick you up from outside your friend's house at a certain time, but give him the address of a well-known red-light district (which he'll be too dim to recognise). Obviously you won't be there and he'll drive slowly up and down the road with his window open, peering at young girls until the police notice him and send a kerb-crawling warning to your home. (Make sure your mother sees it.)

You can start small fires in your bedroom, so your mother will accuse your father of not having paid you sufficient attention and vice versa. Encourage your mother to eat a lot of cake and suet (inject her with lard while she sleeps, if necessary) until she is so fat that your father cannot help comparing her massive, ulcerous ankles to his secretary's dainty little ones. Eventually, he will call her a 'fat cow' and she will leave. But make sure she doesn't get so fat that she can't get out of the door.

TORMENTING YOUR SIBLINGS

BROTHERS AND SISTERS are put on this earth to be teased and made to cry. From the age of five I was expected to share a bedroom with my sister. My mother had given birth to a usurper. I adopted a diet that meant the bedroom was full of toxic fumes, so breathing without gagging was an impossibility. Well done me. I got a bedroom to myself thanks to my bowel problem, while my sister slept on the stairs.

So, if you have a little brother with glasses and a hearing aid, draw attention to his failings and mock him until your mother has to hide his dressing-gown cord. Never forget that asthma can be stress-related and bully him into an attack. Then complain to your parents that it's impossible to do your homework with all that wheezing going on. The sole purpose of having an older brother is that you can lose your virginity to one of his mates. Unfortunately, I didn't have an older brother and none of my older sisters' friends were interested in my clumsy lesbian advances. Good job we had a dog, that's all I can say.

MY SISTER USED very subtle methods to wound me; she was thinner than me, no matter what she ate, so I had a fat arse and she didn't. She wouldn't lend me her clothes, either. One weekend she went away, though, and left behind her purple velvet loon pants. I went on a strict diet, cut down on stealing booze from my parents and was determined to wear those loons at the Friday night Cricket Club disco. I smuggled them out of the house in the morning and hid them in a plastic bag in a hedge. By 8pm I was in the girls' toilets at the Cricket Club, tugging the size 8 loons over my size 14 hips, tucking in the flab as I went along. It was exhausting, my face was the same colour as the pants, but I'd got them on. With one mighty heave I did them up. I have never been in such pain – a roll of puppy fat had got itself firmly caught in the zip. I was torn and bleeding, scarred for life. People still ask how many Caesareans I've had. I bided my time, though, and some years later I found an old photo-booth picture of her pulling a face that looked as though she had learning difficulties. I sent it to a teen magazine, saying that despite her obvious handicap, my sister was a happy and cheerful type of person and that she was a real Kajagoogoo fan.

I won £5 for that letter. My sister was 23 when it was published and trying to be taken seriously as a trainee barrister. When she saw it, she cried for three days. Revenge is sweet.

BEING AN EMBARRASSING PARENT

No. (1)	Date and Place of Birth (2)	Name (if any) (3)	Sex (4)	Name and Surname and Dwelling Place of Father (5)	Name, Surname and Dwelling Place of Mother (6)	Rank or Profession of Father (7)	Signature, Qualification and Residence of Information (8)	When Registered (9)	Signature of Registrar (10)
	1st April 1989 Cinderella's Nite Klub New Cross	Tom William Andrew Timms	Hermaphrodite	Arnold Timms Camberwell Green	**Tom William Andrew Timms**	Godfather Southwark Mafia	Arnold Timms Handman South London	10th April 1989	Valerie Bosman

666 · UNITED KINGDOM

BIRTH CERTIFICATE issued in pursuance of Births and Deaths Registrations Acts 1863 to 1966

Birth registered in the district of Southwark ... the Superintendent Registrar's District of ... in the Country of England

I hereby certify that the foregoing is a true copy of the Entry No. 007 ... in a Register book of Births in my custody.

The Year of Birth in the above Certified Copy is One Thousand 9 Hundred 89

(Superintendent) Registrar of Births and Deaths

Office ... For the District Southwark Date 10th April 1989

TO ALTER OR FUCK ABOUT WITH THIS DOCUMENT OR TO UTTER IT SO ALTERED IS A SERIOUS OFFENCE

THE FAMILY is, of course, a circle. Once you get bored with tormenting your parents and siblings, it's time to expand, start a family of your own; the game needs fresh blood. Let's face it, the only point in having kids is to ritually humiliate them. Start by giving your child a stupid name: for example, a popular option is the place where it was conceived, such as Willesden Green Cemetery, followed by the surname. For bonus points, marry someone called Growcock.

The older a child is, the easier it is to bait. Schooldays can be made miserable by insisting on meeting children at lunchtime in order to breastfeed them through the railings, and wiping their faces in public with gob-soaked hankies. Other mean things are cutting their hair using a pudding basin, packing their lunch boxes with egg sandwiches that smell like farts, being one of those weird families that doesn't have a telly, insisting on

Give your child a longish name, which, when abbreviated down to its initials, spells out T.W.A.T

getting in the bath with them when they'd rather you didn't, talking freely about sex all the time, snogging their dad in front of them, having a shit car and being eligible for free school dinners. One of my greatest ambitions is to put on loads and loads of weight until I weigh fifty-five million billion trillion stone, and then go to my daughter's sports day and run in the mums-and-daughters race in my knickers.

There are so many ways of embarrassing your child – sometimes you do it without even knowing it, which is fantastic. Another personal favourite involves buying the whole family matching shell suits and then marching up and down the High Street, holding hands and singing, 'Kum ba ya, my Lord, Kum ba yah.'

 Book Of Bad Behaviour

CLASS WAR—WHY THE VERY RICH AND THE VERY POOR ARE CHAMPION BAD BEHAVIOURISTS

Life is very unfair. There are those born with a silver spoon up their nostrils, who can get away with murder, whereas common types will be banged up for life because they didn't have a dog licence. Hey ho, I'm glad I'm not really poor and that my sister's a barrister – so useful when I've forgotten to go through the checkout again.

RICH PEOPLE

Abuse Philippinos and have over-developed biceps from constantly throwing bread rolls. I'm particularly keen on 'aristo-prats' because they get away with the most appalling behaviour, just because they own half of Scotland. This seems the best excuse in the world to take loads of heavy drugs and hit coppers. Aristo-prats always use the fact that their parents didn't love them as an excuse to go round causing havoc. No wonder their parents didn't love them, the nasty little gutless inbreds. Posh kids traditionally progress from public school to detox centre, and the reason why they have no morals is that they never had to do a paper round or empty the 'bitty bucket' like I had to. Traditionally, titled families are cursed and have coats of arms featuring syringes and mottos saying stuff like 'weak of chin, weak of heart'. There is very little pure blue blood left in this country, as most of it is tainted with cocaine. Toffs

Weak of chin, weak of heart

have an enormous capacity for low life, they like to mix with pushers, hookers, and people like Fergie. They are born with a chromosome missing, which enables them to shout very poshly without feeling the slightest bit embarrassed.

The thing about rich people is that they can afford to pay for their mistakes, they can trash cars, horses, hotel suites and still come out smirking.

At smart dinner parties, the coke spoon is laid to the left of the soup spoon

13

Jamie Blandford is an icon of bad behaviour to be worshipped and admired by us mealy mouthed lesser mortals.

They're so lucky, imagine how brilliant it would be to smash up a load of really valuable stuff and then just use your best friend's cheque book to replace it.

Mad, rich people are called eccentrics, whereas people on a lesser income would be labelled criminally insane. It's quite OK to take pot-shots at the nanny if you're a member of the House of Lords, whereas if I ask mine to work on a Saturday, I'm up in front of the European Court of Human Rights.

Rich women are born with the ability to differentiate between a tea towel featuring Shire horses and a Hermès silk scarf, which they are just about capable of tying in a knot under their chin (although they frequently need help).

They might not be able to split the atom, but they're terribly good at arranging dried flowers. They are also very useful because they always have the number of a dodgy doctor who will sell you amphetamines. Their Ladyships have children who they send to boarding school as soon as they can crawl, leaving mummy to pursue hobbies such as daytime drinking and fucking the stable hands. Aaah, what a life.

Rich men are incredibly attractive, regardless of the fact that they are congenitally deformed—who cares if you look like a stuffed pike when you've got a big house and servants? This is why you will always see wizened old walruses tottering around with some busty bit of totty hanging off their wallets.

Some badly behaved peers blame their problems on not being cuddled as a child. Errrr, no! Sorry chaps, your problems stem from not being drowned as a child.

The nobility have a wonderful penchant for the dramatic: they are always blowing their inheritance in casinos and crashing around on horses killing small animals and drinking themselves to death. They are the only people in this miserable country who know how to enjoy themselves.

TERRIBLE TODDLERS

MUST MAKE A POINT of smashing their heads against sharp corners in a manner that suggests parental abuse. By 18 months the 'Child of Satan' should have a squint, dummy fixation and rotten teeth from Ribena dependency. By the age of two the Terrible Toddler should have a high tolerance to household cleaning fluids and a preference for cat food. This is the kind of kid that invites incidents with Rotweillers in the park and emerges unscathed whilst the dog lies bleeding on the floor.

The Terrible Toddler will have got the throwing of the tantrum in the supermarket down to a fine art; the child should throw itself under the wheels of a passing trolley and scream until it goes black in the face, so mother has no choice but to beat the living daylights out of it. With any luck there will be a busy body social worker in the queue who will remonstrate with the mother, who'll shove the black-faced one into the social worker's arms and disappear. The Terrible Toddler will then bite the social worker who, taken by surprise, will bite the child back; be reported to the authorities, lose her job, flat, status and eventually commit suicide.The moral of this story is never approach a toddler, especially if it growls.

During this stage of a childs life, attempts will be made to potty train as most nursery schools only accept clean, dry children. The Terrible Toddler will greet any ideas of depriving it of nice, cosy, smelly nappies by depositing turds in mummy's handbag. In desperation, to encourage their incontinent child its parents will take to using the potty themselves and congratulating each other on how clever they are to pooh in it. Unfortunately this becomes such a habit that they forget to use the lavatory when friends come for supper. They'll also expect their visitors to clap and marvel, too. When I was training my daughter she had a novelty potty in the shape of a V.W.Beetle car. The consequence of this, is that every time she gets a lift in a Beetle she dumps on the back seat. It's a reflex action and she can't help it

At the age of three, the Terrible Toddler should embark upon a lifetime's hobby of wasting precious medical resources. It'll start by affecting deafness and short sightedness i.e. gluing itself to the telly and not reacting to sudden loud noises.

15

TRAVEL SICKNESS

AS CHILDREN, my siblings and I had the ability to throw up several times before we reached the end of the drive. My mother's coat collars always reeked of sick and she was forever picking bits of puke out of her cleavage. Being sick is catching, and as soon as my big sister started heaving, I'd join in closely followed by my little brother until the car would be awash with a tidal wave of sick. My mother used to force Travel Sickness pills down our throats—evil smelling little blue tablets which we would immediately regurgitate along with our lunch, necessitating an all over sponge down and a complete change of clothing. That would delay the journey so my dad had to drive like a maniac to reach our destination on time, thus he'd drive dangerously fast round corners, making us throw up even more. I remember the family being asked to leave a motorway service station because we smelt so bad.

Most people eventually grow out of travel sickness but I find that if I eat loads of sweeties, keep the windows shut and try to read a book I can still liven up a dull journey with a nice dramatic honk.

Kids are brilliant at making the drivers life hell, and here are some things you may have forgotten; insist that your sister is taking up more space on the back seat than is fair—start nudging her, then kicking. Build up to gouging out her eyeballs and tearing out her hair. Eventually your father will forget to keep his eyes on the road, turn round and slap you, causing the car to run into a tree. Good, you didn't want to see Great Aunt Kathleen anyway.

Other irritating habits include saying 'how many more miles?' every ten seconds until a main artery explodes in your dad's head, needing a wee wee more times than is humanly possible, (my father refused to take our toilet demands seriously, by his reckoning we might as well be drenched in piss as well as sick. So we were).

When I was young I used to have a 'blanky'. Without it I'd cry and break out in eczema. On really long journey's I'd like to get almost to our destination and then remember I'd forgotten blanky. Dad would have to drive all the way home, only to discover blanky was in the suitcase all the time. Tee hee.

Now that I am grown up, one of my favourite ways of making a trip utterly miserable for everyone is to suddenly decide that I might have left the iron on. I once spent two weeks on a Greek Island whingeing on about it, refusing to relax. Imagine my delight when upon my return I found my home burned down!

Forgetting your passport is another good one—especially if it's supposed to be your honeymoon!

SPOILING CHRISTMAS

CHRISTMAS IS a time of great trauma. Everybody apart from very rich people hate it (they'll give each other Cartier watches and then go skiing, hopefully to somewhere that they'll be engulfed in an avalanche). Every year on Christmas day I like to tell my mother that I'm a lesbian, even though I'm not. It just gets everything going.

The general rule on Christmas day is to start drinking as soon as you have the strength to take the top off the Warninks. It's always better to be a bit pissed whilst opening crap presents because it takes the edge off the disappointment. Christmas started going wrong for me when I was about 14. All I wanted was some clothes, some money, some make-up, some jewellery, some perfume, some platforms, some tights, some electric curlers, a handbag, a leather jacket, a Jackie annual, a selection box, a Pick Of The Pops album featuring a girl on the cover wearing kinky boots full of really bad cover versions, a stereo, a telly for my room and my own front door key. What I actually got was an angle poise lamp so that I didn't strain my eyes whilst I did my homework. My mother ended up with that angle poise lamp—she wore it all Christmas day, tightly wrapped around her neck.

My brother had a 'Christmas face'—basically a sneer as he opened presents which were cheap versions of what he actually wanted. Even now he never opens a gift without asking if you've kept the receipt.

The older I get the more I loathe Christmas, because now I have a horrible family of my own to add to the one which previously scarred me for life.

Xmas means seeing relatives, so a lot of old people who have outlived their savings come round to ponce food off you which they eat with a funny clicking noise. In exchange you get a Christmas present of some second hand cotton buds wrapped up in a bit of Womans Realm.

I can't see the point in making tons of food if people are just going to sit there and eat it. I always buy a Xmas cake from Marks and Spencers which sits in the cupboard looking festive and then is taken back on the 27th and swapped for a new bra.

The way to deal with Christmas of course, is to spoil it so much for everyone that they don't look forward to it next time. Eventually their expectations will be so low that you should be able to get away with spending about £15 on them.

The worst people at Christmas time are the ones that don't spend any money at all, and make everything themselves; cards, wine, food, gifts. Then they chunder on about the true spirit of Christmas which is no excuse for giving you something made out of coat hangers. My mother, in a characteristic demonstration of meanness, once gave all the female members of the family an orange with a load of cloves shoved into it. Apparently this was a pomander and was meant to sweetly scent our knicker drawers which is fine if you like your pants smelling of putrid vegetation. The oranges went mouldy and it took ages to get the spores out of my gussets.

17

HANDY HINTS

IF YOU CAN'T be bothered to buy anything at all, wrap up something that's been lying around the house for ages; a hair band, a pencil or a cassette head-cleaner. Maybe a flannel and some soap; old bits of soap can look brand new if you wrap them in cling film. Another good trick is to get an old book from a junk shop and forge the author's signature – hey presto! A signed first edition. What I tend to do on Christmas Day, is wait for my partner to finish unwrapping all his rubbish gifts, and when he's looking really crestfallen over another tube of Anusol, I shriek, 'Only joking, there's a diamond tie pin somewhere.' Then I make a big fuss of looking for this imaginary gift before it dawns on me that it must have been mixed up in all the wrapping paper that I've just burned in a hastily lit bonfire in the middle of the room. Obviously, this upsets me so much that I cry and cry and cry and have to go to bed for the rest of the day.

Another good way of getting out of Christmas is to fiddle with the fairy lights until you get a massive electric shock. By the time you come round, it will be January and you'll have a nice new hairdo, to boot.

ALL THAT SANTA NONSENSE

I STRONGLY DISAPPROVE of small children being encouraged to sit on some fat bloke's knee, being promised treats if they're good. My Uncle Neville got six months for that kind of behaviour. Make sure you don't forget to inform the under-tens in your house that there is no such thing as Father Christmas. This will also upset any members of your family with Alzheimer's, who might have forgotten that Santa is a fictional character.

HOW TO BEHAVE WITH CAROL SINGERS

PRETEND YOUR NAME IS CAROL SINGER, FOR A LAUGH.
DRESS UP AS ALED JONES – THAT'LL GIVE THEM A SURPRISE.
SPEND DECEMBER SITTING IN THE DARK WITH THE TELLY OFF.
THEN THEY'LL THINK NO-ONE'S IN AND WON'T BOTHER. HA! THAT'S TRICKED THEM, THE IDIOTS.
DON'T GIVE THEM CASH, THEY'LL ONLY SPEND IT DOWN THE 'OFFY'. SAVE THEM THE TRIP—GIVE THEM A LOAD OF FAGS AND BOOZE
INVITE THE CUTE ONE INSIDE FOR SEX

Jenny Eclair's Book Of Bad Behaviour

FESTIVE

I USUALLY GO on a very strict diet over Xmas. This makes everyone else who is stuffing themselves feel like they've got food problems. In fact it's me being a complete twat with half a grapefruit that's the problem. Obviously, I don't give up alcohol on my very strict diet. In fact, drinking on an empty stomach is the most efficient way of getting pissed. Basically, I don't like spending my money on food that disappears down other people's necks, so I make sure that everything I cook is so disgusting that people never want to come to my house again. Christmas dinner is easily ruined by under-cooking the turkey by several hours, so that it bleeds dramatically all over the table. I also have a habit of mistaking the bottle of washing-up liquid for brandy and liberally dousing the pudding in lemon squeezy. This has the added fun factor of making people foam at the mouth, whereupon I phone the relevant authorities and have everyone taken away and put in quarantine, leaving me in peace to masturbate over my new Take That annual.

HOW TO BEHAVE AT YOUR CHILD'S NATIVITY PLAY

1. SIT STONY-FACED, WHILE ALL THE OTHER MUMS WEEP INTO THEIR HANKIES.

2. COMPLAIN ABOUT THE LACK OF PROFESSIONALISM AND LOUDLY REMARK THAT AT LEAST MACAULEY CULKIN WOULDN'T HAVE WET HIS PANTS.

3. HECKLE THE INN KEEPER FOR HAVING A CRAP ACCENT.

4. BOO AT THE END.

5. INSIST ON A THEATRICAL AGENT TO NEGOTIATE YOUR CHILD'S FEE.

6. OFFER A PROFESSIONAL VIDEO SERVICE AT A COMPETITIVE RATE. MAKE SURE THE END PRODUCT SHOWS ONLY CLOSE-UPS OF YOUR KIDDIE.

7. TAKE ON THE ROLE OF DIRECTOR. GO BACKSTAGE AFTERWARDS AND GIVE THE CHILDREN NOTES.

8. WRITE A SCATHING REVIEW IN THE LOCAL PAPER.

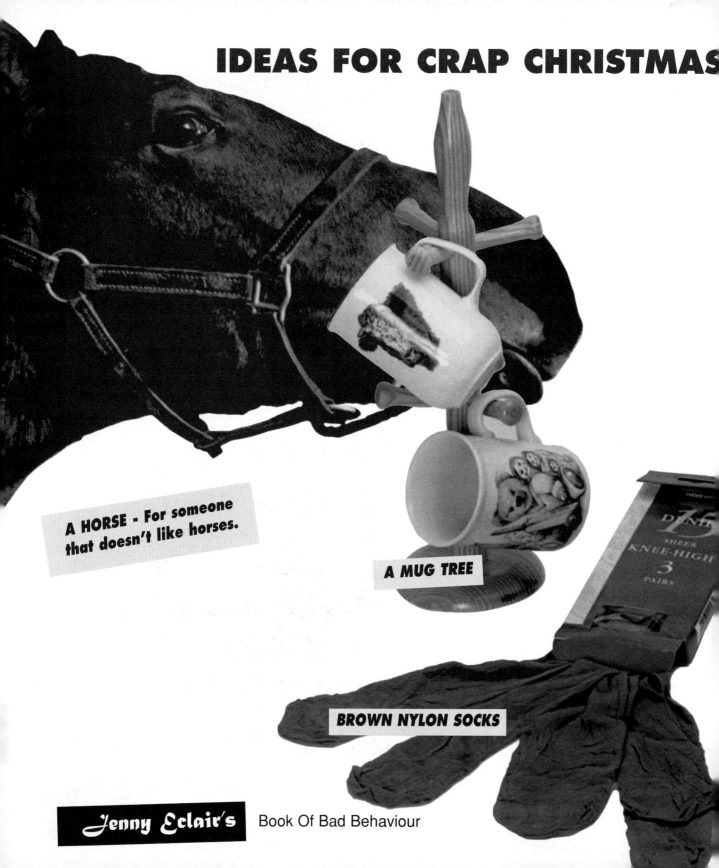

PRESENTS.

A BUMPER PACK OF TOILET ROLLS - These will look impressive wrapped up in festive paper

A STATUETTE

SAINSBURY'S
Supersoft
LUXURY BATHROOM TISSUE
SOFT WHITE

A GNOME

BATTERIES - But no game

A BOWL TO PUT SAVOURY SNACKS IN

SCOURING PADS

EMERY BOARDS

21

PROBLEM CHILDREN

AT FIVE years old you will be required by law to go to school. The problem child has several options here: go, and be the class bully; develop asthma and be too poorly to go; pretend to go but spend the day hiding in a tree; or burn the school down. Starting school is a good time to demonstrate your inner torment by bed wetting (actually bed wetting is fine at any time, especially if like me, you can't be arsed to get up in the middle of the night and go to the toilet). Constant sheet changing is exhausting for any mother (particularly if, as in my mum's case, she's over 60).

School is a great place for the problem child to spread its tyranny a bit further and bring misery to those outside the immediate family. The problem child never does that badly at school because the form teacher will lie about its progress rather than face the possibility of dealing with it for another twelve months should it be held back a year. In fact, at my primary school, all the teachers got together and forged my examination results in the hope that they could shunt me off into secondary education by the time I was seven. Eventually, my father joined the army which was the best possible excuse for me having to change schools so many times. The best thing about school is that it provides you with an arsenal of weaponry with which you can inflict pain on other people: rulers, Biros, elastic bands, drawing-pins – all these things are good, but compasses are best, because you can use them to give yourself a home-made tattoo or for stabbing people. To this day I still tool myself up with a compass when I go out at night; if I get stopped by the police I say that I'm a graphic designer.

There are many ways to be a problem child: it doesn't have to be a cliché of glue sniffing, illiteracy and petty thieving; you can cause as much grief by showing signs of becoming an uptight little arsehole. The more trendy and liberal your parents are, the more effective this is. You can be a massive disappointment to your Bohemian mum and dad if you demand Laura Ashley wallpaper and hand-smocked dresses (unless you are a boy, of course, in which case they'd be delighted at the anti-macho stance). Be rabidly anti-smoking and tut over the number of empty wine bottles. Finally, you can stitch them up by informing the police about your father's funny 'tomato' plants. I ration my daughter's Blue Peter viewing in case she turns into a rather nice, dull person. It's not that I'd encourage her to shoplift, but if she could get me a Paloma Picasso lipstick or some of that Kinnebo make-up that all the super models wear, then I'd only tell her off a bit. But if she whined about how much gin I drank, I'd slap her legs.

 **Book Of Bad Behaviour**

HALLOWE'EN

HALLOWE'EN HAS gotten completely out of hand. I blame the greetings card manufacturers who will not rest until we have to buy a poxy card every day of the year. The only good thing about Hallowe'en is going up to ugly people and screaming like you're really scared and saying, 'Take the mask off. Take the mask off...'

On Hallowe'en night I am always well prepared for the local kiddies that think I don't know that they do stupid impressions of me behind my back. What I do is make up little bags of sherbet dip, consisting mostly of soap powder, and I give them gob stoppers which are in fact real bull's eyes. It's quite something to see a five-year-old struggling with the chewy optic nerve, and is just punishment for them leaving piles of green gob on my car. Another good trick is to buy some large pumpkins which can be dropped from an upstairs window onto unwelcome callers.

BONFIRE NIGHT
(ANYTHING THAT UPSETS ANIMALS IS FINE BY ME)

BONFIRE NIGHT IS a great time to behave in a thoroughly idiotic fashion: the combination of alcohol and explosives will guarantee you a good time. The trouble with most fireworks that you can buy from shops is that they are feeble. However, I know this bloke, Irish chappie, who can make really good fireworks with just a bit of petrol and a few old milk bottles. It is really good having a bonfire in your garden because with any luck it will get out of hand and you'll be able to call out the fire brigade, legitimately for once. And you know how I feel about firemen: basically they were put on this earth so that women of a certain age can just shut their eyes, visualise the uniform, and have a belting orgasm.

There is something very sexy about bonfire night. I think it's got something to do with men and women going 'ooh' and 'ah' together that does it. I also find the glow of a bonfire very flattering to my complexion. And, I'm afraid, being a bit tragic, I enjoy writing my name with sparklers. What I can't be doing with on November the fifth are community firework displays where people congregate in some park and have to stand behind barriers whilst someone with asbestos gloves tits around being cautious. If no-one was hideously scarred as a result of the old Catherine wheel spinning off the wall, then there'd be no-one weird-looking to stare at on the bus.

PARTIES

OBVIOUSLY, BECAUSE I AM A SOCIAL LEPER, I do not get invited to parties that often. Doesn't stop me going though, gatecrashing is all part of the fun. You know what it's like, you walk past a house, you hear music and laughter, you just have to go in. Which is how I ended up spending last Saturday afternoon at an extremely tedious 3rd birthday party. I wouldn't have minded but I didn't win anything.

CHILDREN'S PARTIES WHAT A NIGHTMARE!

These are best avoided. What I try and do is attempt to blow up a few balloons, and because I smoke so much my lungs collapse, so off I go to hospital smiling and waving. Here are some others ways that you can spoil your child's birthday party...

FORGET TO HAND OUT THE INVITATIONS

THERE IS NOTHING like seeing a child dressed up in party regulation lacey tights and black patent shoes (boys too) with its face pressed up against the window waiting for chums that will not turn up. All because their invites are lying at the bottom of your handbag, along with all those tampons that have come unwrapped and are covered in bits of fluff but may be useful in an emergency.

GETTING THE FOOD WRONG

KIDS EXPECT THE usual stuff like sandwiches and crisps and mini rolls and jelly and ice cream and sausages and cheese and pineapple on sticks.
Give them sushi, they're going to be sick anyway. By the way, when any child is sick in my house I make sure they mop it up themselves, because if I do it I start honking.

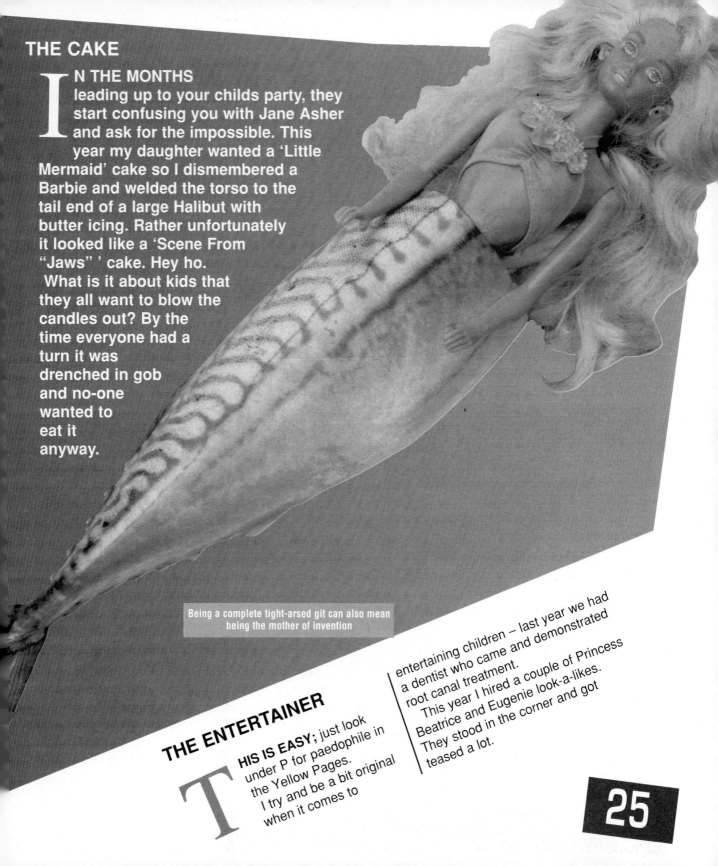

THE CAKE

IN THE MONTHS leading up to your childs party, they start confusing you with Jane Asher and ask for the impossible. This year my daughter wanted a 'Little Mermaid' cake so I dismembered a Barbie and welded the torso to the tail end of a large Halibut with butter icing. Rather unfortunately it looked like a 'Scene From "Jaws"' cake. Hey ho. What is it about kids that they all want to blow the candles out? By the time everyone had a turn it was drenched in gob and no-one wanted to eat it anyway.

Being a complete tight-arsed git can also mean being the mother of invention

THE ENTERTAINER

THIS IS EASY; just look under P for paedophile in the Yellow Pages. I try and be a bit original when it comes to entertaining children – last year we had a dentist who came and demonstrated root canal treatment.

This year I hired a couple of Princess Beatrice and Eugenie look-a-likes. They stood in the corner and got teased a lot.

THE PARTY BAG

THESE HAVE GOT completely out of hand, it's all so competitive. They all expect tickets to Euro Disney or backstage passes to the next Take That concert. It's just too expensive. But now I've got it sussed. You know those gas-fired disposable lighters? Well, you can get four of those for a quid in the market. Easy—balloon, piece of cake, lighter – now bugger off.

Actually, I find children's parties are the best way of finding out who's parents have got the most cash. Kids that bring really cheap rubbish gifts like a Polly Pocket fun palace made out of a McDonalds carton should be discouraged, as the chances of your brat being asked to spend the entire summer holidays in their Tuscan farmhouse are nil.

De-luxe party bags include 20 Capstan Full Strength

Haven't got a clue. They should have all their money confiscated for being so crap. Really rich people don't carry cash, because its dirty and a bus conductor might have touched it. The Nouveau Riche think that if they give a lot of money to charity they will make the New Years Honours List. They are the only people in the world who still get a hard on thinking about going to the Palace to pick up an M.B.E.

Wives of the Nouveau Riche take elocution lessons but still say 'toilet' and 'serviette'. The stress of giving formal dinner parties for Japanese clients give them a nervous tic and a Valium addiction. Any day now they'll get caught shop lifting in which case they must do the honourable thing and throw themselves down the waste disposal unit.

Their kids are in that horrible situation of being the only kids at nob school called Kimberly-Anne and Trev. Nouveau Riche people live in mock Tudor mansions and are terrified of the housekeeper who despises them for eating dinner at lunchtime. They are forever giving the cook the day off so they can eat fried spam sandwiches and tinned peaches with Carnation milk. The N. R. fake liking olives in an attempt to be sophisticated and say things like,'What's your poison?' They all have games rooms but pretend they don't play darts. Some of them build their own Golf courses, but this is only because the local Golf Club won't let them join.

The Nouveau Riche think it's smart to have cocktail bars that light up and play Chas and Dave numbers

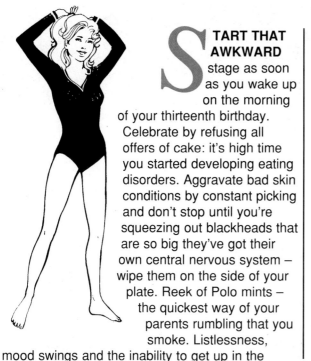

START THAT AWKWARD stage as soon as you wake up on the morning of your thirteenth birthday. Celebrate by refusing all offers of cake: it's high time you started developing eating disorders. Aggravate bad skin conditions by constant picking and don't stop until you're squeezing out blackheads that are so big they've got their own central nervous system – wipe them on the side of your plate. Reek of Polo mints – the quickest way of your parents rumbling that you smoke. Listlessness, mood swings and the inability to get up in the morning are all part of growing up; they are also the symptoms of solvent abuse and will worry your parents sick.

If you are a girl, have underage sex, get pregnant and insist it's appendicitis, even when the head's showing. Give birth at school – that'll liven up maths and maybe even get you out of PE. Not at my school, however, which was very strict and chivvied girls out onto the hockey pitch before they'd even managed to expel the placenta. Remember, your sole intention is to get yourself into council care, where you can drink cider and have sex with your social worker.

All teenage girls are obsessed by their looks. Every adolescent girl will look in the mirror one day and think, 'I wonder what I'd look like without any eyebrows?' (Pluck, pluck, shave, shave, and you look like shit.) Not only do you look like shit, you look surprised that you look like shit.

The teen years are the time to experiment with clothes. This is so that in years to come, when you

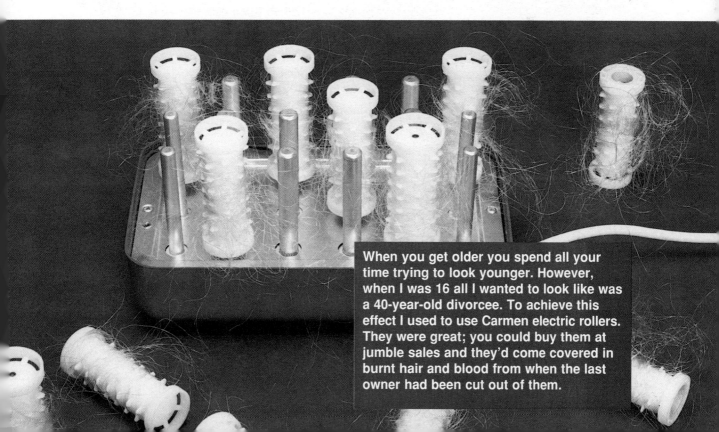

When you get older you spend all your time trying to look younger. However, when I was 16 all I wanted to look like was a 40-year-old divorcee. To achieve this effect I used to use Carmen electric rollers. They were great; you could buy them at jumble sales and they'd come covered in burnt hair and blood from when the last owner had been cut out of them.

are a sad thirtysomething and your life is over, you can look at your old photo albums and laugh out loud. I was a teenager in the Seventies and spent most of the decade in and out of hospital, thanks to fashion-induced accidents. You'd think that having fractured my ankles several times nearly twenty years ago, I'd have the sense not to wear platforms (or Spaz boots, as we used to call them) a second time around. Sadly not. As I write this, I am wearing a rather grubby elastic bandage around my left ankle. Last week, I fell, when pissed, off the pavement. As I went crashing down it was with a feeling of *déjà vu*. Puff-sleeved blouses were also very trendy in those days. You had to be careful with the puff-sleeved blouse: one false move and you'd be down the disco with half a shepherds' pie hanging off your wrist.

When I was a teenager, some people of my age would pretend to be hippies. You could smell these people before you could see them because they wore stinky Afghan coats. I had a friend whose mum sewed one of those toilet-freshener blocks into the lining; she was also the kind of mum who ironed a neat crease down the middle of his jeans. He was a laughing stock; he was also my boyfriend. Going out with unsuitable people is all part of the learning process; all middle-class girls cannot resist a bit of low life. I used to hang out at a bikers' café when I was fifteen. My parents despaired. I had a boyfriend called Slug and had to pretend to like heavy metal music (secretly I was still a David Cassidy fan). My parents hated me going to this café, but instead of banning me, they did something much cleverer: They encouraged me to go. They'd give me lifts down there and say things like, 'Oh that looks fun, shall we pop in for a coffee? We could meet some of your new friends.' I stopped going. The moral of this story is always lie to your parents about where you are going, because if they ever find you taking blow-backs off some greasy dealer, they'll kill you. Actually, it's much

Who wants to go out with the boy next door when this kind of big trouser action's loose on the streets?

Jenny Eclair's Book Of Bad Behaviour

cleverer to smoke pot in the public library because if your mum and dad do catch you, they're not allowed to shout on the premises.

Teenage boys, of course, are equally difficult, but smell worse. They also wank all the time. All of a sudden those Airfix kits just aren't as much fun any more and they wake up in the morning thinking, 'What have I got to do today? Oh yes, have a wank.'

It's not surprising that a man invented penicillin: it was in a pair of his underpants underneath the bed all the time.

Bad hygiene is de rigueur for the teenager: refuse to change your socks until you develop trench foot (a great excuse for time off school); neglect your teeth so they go brown. This will make people think that you're taking loads of cheap speed and, therefore, are really cool and trendy. No self-respecting teenager ever stands up straight; what we're after is seriously bad posture which will eventually lead to a curvature of the spine. (Good, even more time off school.)

Finally, don't forget to steal money out of your mother's purse. This is a habit you must never grow out of: I still do it and I'm over 30. In fact, these days, when they go on holiday, I burgle their house. People say, 'How could you?' I say, 'Easy, I know where the spare keys are hidden.'

TEENAGE PARTIES

WHAT BLISS. Remember when your parents didn't realise that cider was alcoholic and they trusted you for the very first time to have boys round and 'not be silly'? How you abused that trust! And then they came back early and everyone was naked and your dad got the police because two lads from the secondary modern had arrived on Honda 50s. Well, my parents were never that stupid. I had to go to other people's houses in order to have sex on a heap of coats, which was a really anti-social habit back in the Seventies because suedette was in fashion and it's really hard to get spunk stains out of suedette, I can tell you. Then I'd have to get home and pretend not to be drunk, and my parents would be sitting up waiting for me, pretending not to be drunk, and everyone would talk really slowly and carefully about what a pleasant evening we'd had. I remember coming home from a party when I was

31

about sixteen and I was ridiculously drunk because home-made beer-brewing kits had just come on the market and my friend's dad had a dustbin-full in the airing cupboard. I had to leave early because I was farting so dramatically as a result. Anyway, I got in, negotiated the stairs, put myself to bed and lay there knowing that I had 100 per cent chance of throwing up. I couldn't use the bathroom because my parents would hear. There was only one thing for it. In the bottom drawer of my wardrobe I kept all my old back copies of *Jackie*, which I was sure would be worth a fortune one day. I opened the drawer and emptied the contents of my body into it, then shut the drawer firmly and went to sleep dreaming schoolgirl dreams of going down on Woody from the Bay City Rollers.

It was three weeks before my mother went out for long enough for me to get rid of the evidence, during which time I wasted all my talc trying to keep the odious stench at bay.

According to my parents, teenage parties in their day were full of girls and boys who played tennis together and drank fruit punch and there was never any of that daft necking nonsense. I will probably try the same thing on with my daughter, though there is diary evidence to prove I did otherwise. Here is an entry from my 1977 Lett's *Diary for Girl Guides* (my mother never accepted that I'd been chucked out): 'Went to a party at Maz's house. Got really smashed on Martini, snogged Gaz and Andy P. Then Baz arrived with Chaz. I went with Chaz for a bit but then I ended up in the bedroom with Maz. Came home via the golf links with Baz. I think he's nicer than Gaz but I still love Gaz.' The entry for the following day just reads, 'Today I had a very sore vagina.'

ADULT PARTIES

YOU KNOW YOU'RE getting old when the prospect of going to a party that doesn't have food no longer appeals. I have a theory about food at parties: no matter how much French bread you buy, there will always be twice as much left over in the morning. When I was younger I thought that a good party consisted of dancing to Radio Caroline while a boy with fur round his anorak hood switched the lights on and off. I thought that there could be nothing duller than a grown-ups' party. This is not the case: we are grown-up; we can afford more booze and more drugs; our records are better and considering the fact that most of us are in long-term relationships, the prospect of a grope on the stairs with a stranger is that much more exciting. Whenever I go to a party I deposit my bottle of Thunderbird in the kitchen and go off in search of the airing cupboard. In my experience, particularly at student parties, the hard stuff is always hidden in the airing cupboard. It is also worth remembering that whenever there is a meeting of a religious nature there will always be a bottle of sherry knocking around. Sherry is great because it's a necessary ingredient for my favourite dish, the fat-free trifle in which there is no custard, bits of old sponge or banana. In fact, it's just a cut-glass dish containing sherry. At my house this is traditionally eaten with a straw and makes a refreshing alternative to cornflakes.

The best grown-up parties happen when you combine the ingredients of a children's party and a teenage party with the sophisticated elements of an adult party (like having toilet paper in the bathroom). Games like Twister are wasted on kids, who just don't get the sexual connotations of sprawling around with your left leg on the blue dot and your right knee on the yellow. On the other hand, it is a brilliant game to drag out of

The alternative sherry trifle

the cupboard at grown-up parties, because you will get a big thrill having a legitimate excuse, at last, to get marriage-breakingly intimate with your best friend's husband. Other good games include passing oranges under the chin and playing blind man's buff with a difference. The difference being that everyone takes their clothes off, apart from the person in the blindfold, who runs around trying to guess who people are by touching up their privates. At teenage parties there is always a girl crying in the corner. This is even better when it's a 35-year-old whose husband has walked out on her and she's just realised that her future lies in B&B accommodation somewhere in Croydon. Grown-up

parties are always fraught with sexual tension, because so and so's ex has just turned up with so and so. This is made even more intriguing if there has been a change of sexual preference somewhere along the line. The only drawback to entertaining adults is the amount of babies that have a habit of turning up too. These babies are normally strapped into carry cots, which are then shoved under a table. Many's the time I have woken up after a party at my house only to find amongst the wreckage, hundreds of sticks of stale French bread plus a few forgotten babies, who just lie there, chewing unwanted crusts, until they are reclaimed.

BADLY BEHAVED PEOPLE AND THEIR + HEALTH!

 Book Of Bad Behaviour

HEAVY DRINKING

A LOT OF MEN get very funny about women drinking: they don't really like it. Well, I'm sorry lads, but if we didn't get pissed, most of you would never get a shag. That's where the problem lies. Personally, I think alcohol should be subject to the same kind of government health warnings that fags are. You buy a bottle of sangria, you need a label on the side reading, 'WARNING, DRINKING THIS COULD MAKE YOU SLEEP WITH SOMEONE WHO LOOKS AS THOUGH THEY LIVE UNDER A CARPET.'

We've all been there (too many bloody times). Many of us worry about the amount we drink. This is because alcohol makes you paranoid and because the guidelines on safe drinking only make sense if you translate the word 'unit' into 'bucket'.

People who behave badly are never very well. This is because they drink and smoke too much and go out without wearing a vest. They are also more inclined to suffer other maladies such as the septic love bite, genital warts, broken limbs, depression, beriberi, scurvy, hepatitis, brittle nails and diarrhoea. The most common ailment of the badly behaved person is the HANGOVER. This is a wasting disease, because people who are suffering from a hangover will waste an entire day waiting to feel like a normal human being again. Hangovers are the result of ALCOHOL ABUSE.

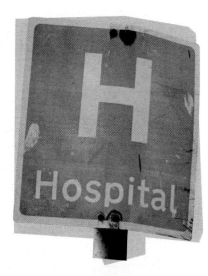

YOU KNOW YOU DRINK TOO MUCH WHEN...

- YOU FINISH THAT CAN OF LAGER YOU'VE BEEN USING AS AN ASHTRAY
- YOU ARE 38 YEARS OLD AND YOU STILL WET THE BED
- YOU DON'T COUNT SPARKLING WHITE WINE AS ALCOHOL
- YOU SPILL YOUR PINT AND SUCK THE CARPET
- YOU LAUGH AT HALE AND PACE
- YOUR BEST FRIENDS LIVE IN THE PARK
- YOU HAVE YOUR OWN SET OF YARD O ALE GLASSES FOR EVERY DAY USE
- YOU PUMP YOUR OWN STOMACH SO THAT YOU CAN START AGAIN
- YOU FIND IT EASIER TO OPEN A CAN OF RED STRIPE THAN BOIL A KETTLE
- YOU TURN INTO A FISH
- YOU ONLY BUY POTATOES TO MAKE WHISKY
- YOU DRINK PORT TO QUENCH YOUR THIRST
- BLACKBIRDS MISTAKE YOUR NOSE FOR A GIANT STRAWBERRY
- YOU CAN'T FOR THE LIFE OF YOU REMEMBER YOUR NAME
- YOU FIND YOURSELF IN THE PERFUMERY DEPARTMENT OF JOHN LEWIS SWIGGING THE TESTERS
- IF YOU'VE GOT NOTHING ELSE TO MIX WITH ORANGE JUICE THEN NAIL VARNISH IS PERFECTLY ACCEPTABLE
- YOU GO TO FRANCE ON A CHEAP AWAYDAY WITH A LOAD OF SUN READERS JUST TO STOCK UP ON BOOZE
- THE GIRL ON THE SUPERMARKET CHECKOUT ASKS IF YOU'RE HAVING A PARTY, WHEN ALL YOU'VE BOUGHT IS ENOUGH FOR A NIGHT IN BY YOURSELF
- YOU HAVE TO PHONE YOUR FRIENDS IN THE MORNING TO FIND OUT WHAT YOU DID THE NIGHT BEFORE, BUT THEY WON'T SPEAK TO YOU

So how many did you tick? I ticked them all, thereby scoring maximum points and declaring myself Champion Piss-head.

 Book Of Bad Behaviour

ALCOHOL - the side effects

EVEN MORE EMBARRASSING than pissing yourself in public and the one thing that makes me seriously consider going on the wagon, is the amount of shit poetry that I write when I'm drunk.

Physically, I cannot take my drink and I'm always covered in bruises from falling off tables. Seriously, though, alcohol almost blinded me once: I came home, completely off my face, I took out my contact lenses and collapsed, unconscious, on the bathroom floor. I came round about five hours later, covered in shame, humiliation, and sick. I thought to myself, 'Now I must take out my contact lenses.' It's always harder a second time around, ripping off your retinas.

Alcohol can, of course, make you hideously fat, but I find that if I don't eat any food I can use up the spare calories on booze. Also, I find that drinking on an empty stomach has much quicker results and is therefore much more cost effective. For many years people have been advised to line their stomach with milk before a heavy session. Time after time I have disproved this theory: drinking a pint of full-cream milk means that you have to double the amount of alcohol it usually takes to have you offering strangers oral sex in the gents' toilet of your local pub. Now, where's the sense in that, eh?

I have been drinking for many years now, and the only time I ever gave up for a reasonable length of time was when I was pregnant: I was bored out of my skull for nine months and this probably has something to do with why I only have one child.

Unfortunately, years of drinking takes its toll and these days I get hangovers. The hangover is the body's way of preparing you for old age. Did you know that in Japan you can get this virtual-reality kit which gives you the sensation of being extremely old? Your vision goes and you find it difficult to speak or walk. Of course, it costs a billion quid and is a complete waste of money considering you could get the same effect by re-introducing the Party 7.

Kids and hangovers don't mix because they just don't understand that mummy is about to die, so they come in playing their recorder and asking you to do simple things, which at that moment you have about as much chance of achieving as Stephen Hawking has of competing an Olympic decathlon. Let me give you an example: I am over thirty; I am hungover to the teeth. My five-year-old comes in and expects me to find her shoe. Listen, I cannot look for her shoe – if I bend over I will black out. This is how I deal with the situation: 'Shoe? Shoe? I don't know where your bloody shoe is, and what's more I don't care. You can just hop for the rest of your life as far as I'm concerned.'

In years to come, my daughter is going to write a book entitled *My Mother: The Alcoholic Old Bitch* and it will serve me right.

37

AN UNHAPPY START TO THE NEW YEAR

ON NEW YEARS EVE you can enter strange people's houses on the pretext of 'first footing'. All you need for this is a blackened face and a lump of coal, although I find a house brick and a balaclava more effective. Once you're in, don't leave. Everyone will think you're a friend of that peculiar cousin who nobody remembers meeting before 1989, when he turned up the doorstep calling everyone 'auntie' and 'uncle'.

New Year's Eve is a time to make a huge list of resolutions and resolutely smash them by 1.30am. on the 1st. Breaking New Year's resolutions is a great game to play with your mates. Each of you should make up ten resolutions and then compete as to who can break all theirs first. Things like giving up smoking and chocolate are simply smashed by finishing off the Quality Street on New Year's Day while simultaneously smoking 40 fags. I lost points one year, however, by resolving to give up shoplifting and then having to wait 24 hours before Marks & Spencer reopened after the holiday.

BAR MITZVAHS

THIS IS A JEWISH BASH celebrating the rite of passage from boy to manhood. The 13-year-old youth in question has to wear a cuppel, otherwise known as 'one of those funny little hats'. He must then recite a big chunk of the Koran in Hebrew and then fart into a milk bottle. Then, and only then, is he a man. Actually, I think a boy becomes a man when his penis reaches a sufficient size to satisfy a woman, in which case most of these boys would have to wait a very long time: 13-year-olds still sit on the top deck of a bus and pretend to be the driver, for heaven's sake.

The female equivalent of the bar mitzvah, is the bat mitzvah, which, thanks to the strange combination of religious zealots and feminism, is becoming more popular. It might also have something to do with lots of 13-year-old girls getting pissed off at losing out on pressies such as Gameboys and CD players. A bar mitzvah is traditionally held on a Saturday; the feast is held on the next day and involves all things bar bits of pig. I don't know about you, but whenever I get invited to a bar mitzvah I always keep a pork pie in my pocket and for some reason talk incessantly about pullovers.

MAKING A MOCKERY OUT OF EASTER

ON EASTER SUNDAY you should go to church for the first time in your life and regurgitate chocolate all over the pew. I think it's a terrible shame that the religious connotations of Easter have been buried under a tide of commercialism and cocoa extracts. What have bunnies and eggs got to do with Jesus dying on the cross? Surely it would be more apt if we stuffed ourselves with chocolate crucifixes, complete with novelty choc sons of Our Lord, possibly with a crown of green fondant icing and a soft-centre head filled with raspberry liqueur.

Some people really get into Easter and start doing things like decorating bits of pussy willow with painted hens' eggs and making simnel cakes. But really, could you be arsed? Children, of course, get all stupid about it and think they might get more exciting things than just chocolate, which they have every day now that it's not rationed, but I find that nailing them to the shed door for a few hours soon shuts them up. Crucifixion is a brilliant form of punishment and should be implemented in all secondary schools.

SOME NEW YEAR'S RESOLUTIONS I HAVE BROKEN

- ✗ STOP MASTURBATING OVER TAKE THAT
- ✗ GET MY OWN CHANNEL 4 SERIES
- ✗ WRITE A SOPHISTICATED COMEDY BOOK
- ✗ LIKE NANETTE NEWMAN
- ✗ RESPECT THE COMEDY TALENTS OF HUGH LAURIE
- ✗ ALLOW MY NATURAL HAIR COLOUR TO GROW OUT
- ✗ STOP FARTING
- ✗ USE NATURAL SPONGES RATHER THAN TAMPONS
- ✗ GIVE MONEY TO ANIMAL CHARITIES
- ✗ STOP APPLYING FOR A JOB ON THE WORD
- ✗ COME CLEAN ABOUT MY AGE
- ✗ STOP PRESSING MYSELF UP AGAINST STRANGE YOUNG MEN WHEN THE SPACE ISN'T CONFINED ENOUGH TO WARRANT IT

1 January

39

(SPEND A DAY IN A PRECINCT - LOTS OF SCOPE TO BE APPALLING UNDER ONE ROOF)

I LOVE TO GO shopping. Correction: I prefer shoplifting because it's cheaper. I used to be much better at nicking stuff, but my eyesight is failing and I can't run as fast as I could. Also, I've been caught a couple of times and it tends to put you off. And I worry about the sort of stuff that I steal these days. I got really depressed the other week when I realised that I'd pinched a load of tea towels – I really am getting old and dull. I used to steal clothes: what I did was go into Chelsea Girl looking like a normal size 12 and come out weighing 45 stone. When questioned, I told the store detective that due to poor circulation I had to wear eighteen layers of clothing; she didn't believe me and I was taken home in a police car, whereupon my father shot himself on the lawn.

I also remember attempting to thieve a packet of chewing gum from the rack next to the till. Unfortunately, the button on my jacket got caught in the wire rack and I had to run through Blackpool with this wire rack full of sweeties bouncing off my chest, followed by people shouting, 'stop, thief'. I also nicked a lot of key rings. I don't know why, I didn't have any keys – do you think my parents were stupid enough to give their front door key to a daughter with a criminal record?

I had a specially adapted shoplifting coat – I slit the pockets in my school mac so that when I shoved stuff into them, the contraband would fall through into the lining and bounce around the bottom of the hem. I was always heavily bruised at this time from constantly having hundreds of stolen Cadbury's Creme Eggs bouncing around my kneecaps.

To shoplift well, you mustn't have a conscience. We used to go round in a gang and the person who spoilt it for everyone was the one that got a pang of guilt and was caught, trying clumsily to replace a pair of earrings she'd pinched the day before. Silly cow. This time the woman was awake.

People often blame juvenile delinquency on the parents. I blame it on shops for stocking nice little things that you can just slip into the palm of you hand and walk out with.

Shoplifting isn't the only naughty thing to do in shops: if you're a bit chicken, there are some other ideas on page 42.

As a teenager, running out of shops with things like this clamped between my knees, under my dress, has affected the way I walk today.

THE LOWER MIDDLE CLASSES

Are far too wet to behave really badly. Anyway, they don't have time: they're too busy

underwear hygiene...

queuing in the Post Office buying TV licences. The lower middle classes are conservative; they worry about being noticed and will eat raw liver in restaurants rather than cause a scene. Lower middle class people swear by Marks & Spencer (actually they don't swear at all and if they say 'sod it', they make a donation to Dr Barnado's). They are obsessed with clean underwear, whereas rich people don't care

about monstrous skid marks because they know you'll sleep with them anyway.

Demographically, the lower middle classes are most likely to be virgins on their wedding night. That's how dull they are.

They have an over-developed sense of guilt and will hand themselves over to the police if they accidentally use an out-of-date bus pass. These are the type of people who return their library books. They also put their spectacles back in the case and wash the car on a Sunday morning while everyone else is having sex. Lower middle class people drink tea with their evening meal and

enjoy a 'nice chop' (personally I don't think there is any such thing as a nice chop). They worry about new-fangled things such as courgettes and have never seen their partner naked. Lower middle class people do not approve of divorce and would rather stay together for forty years, not speaking, until one of them cracks and attacks the other with a meat cleaver. Being a pillar of society can be enormously frustrating and that's why these people tend to go berserk. Most serial killers are from the ranks of the lower middle class, and it's always the dullest of suburban back gardens which get dug up to reveal rotting corpses. Ultimately, the lower middle classes are the most deviant. That's why they have net curtains; they have things to hide, the weirdos. These are the kind of people who join the Territorial Army.

. . .a lower middle class obsession!

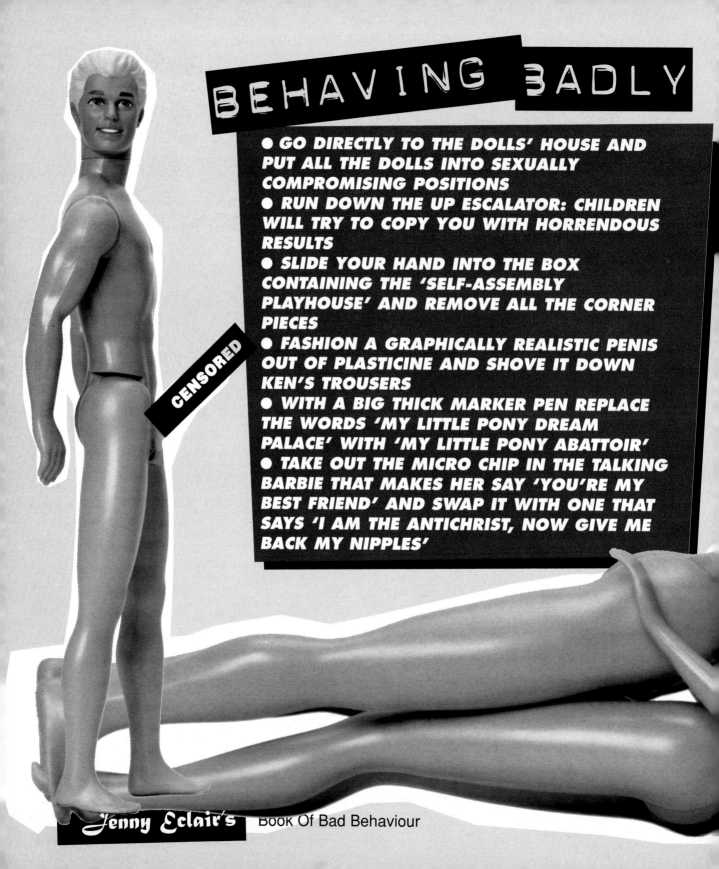

BEHAVING BADLY

- GO DIRECTLY TO THE DOLLS' HOUSE AND PUT ALL THE DOLLS INTO SEXUALLY COMPROMISING POSITIONS
- RUN DOWN THE UP ESCALATOR: CHILDREN WILL TRY TO COPY YOU WITH HORRENDOUS RESULTS
- SLIDE YOUR HAND INTO THE BOX CONTAINING THE 'SELF-ASSEMBLY PLAYHOUSE' AND REMOVE ALL THE CORNER PIECES
- FASHION A GRAPHICALLY REALISTIC PENIS OUT OF PLASTICINE AND SHOVE IT DOWN KEN'S TROUSERS
- WITH A BIG THICK MARKER PEN REPLACE THE WORDS 'MY LITTLE PONY DREAM PALACE' WITH 'MY LITTLE PONY ABATTOIR'
- TAKE OUT THE MICRO CHIP IN THE TALKING BARBIE THAT MAKES HER SAY 'YOU'RE MY BEST FRIEND' AND SWAP IT WITH ONE THAT SAYS 'I AM THE ANTICHRIST, NOW GIVE ME BACK MY NIPPLES'

CENSORED

Jenny Eclair's Book Of Bad Behaviour

ESPECIALLY IN A TOY SHOP!

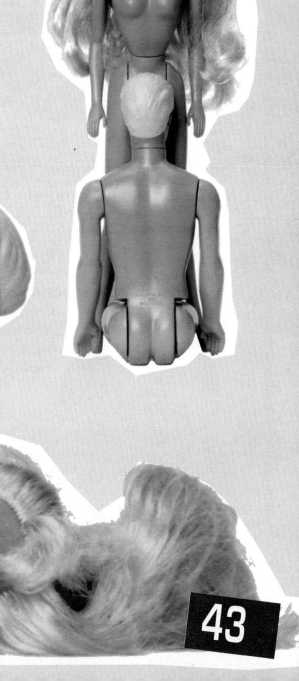

43

AKA THE GREAT DEPRESSION

SO, YOU'VE GOT this far. You might have a degree, you might not – it doesn't matter, you're never going to get a job, anyway. You're a loser. This is the time in your life when it's fun to play at being a 'national statistic', so pander to every right-wing bigoted preconception. Live off the state and Pot Noodles, sleep in your underwear, get a council flat, satellite telly, have loads of kids and hit them. If they don't cry enough, swap them for ones which do. Fill your garden with scrap metal. God, what a brilliant way to live! By now you should have a criminal record. If you've forgotten to get one, go out now and punch a

Keep loads of Alsatians that crap everywhere. If they don't crap more than your neighbours' dogs, take them back to the pet shop and demand some that crap more

copper. If you've not managed a prison sentence, pretend you have – doing a stretch is the best way to avoid gainful employment. Remember, all old lags wear a cheap blue suit with very wide lapels that doesn't really fit. Suggesting that you went down in the Seventies and have only just got out.

Women in their twenties should start letting themselves go. Heroin speeds up this process, as does constantly being up the duff. Go for the ravaged look; bleach your hair and let the roots grow out, have bare white legs and wear short skirts with battered stilettoes. Go to bingo all the time, become a loan-shark victim and adopt a Liverpudlian accent. Obviously it's tiring being a cliché, some people get bored, stop concentrating and the next thing they know they're managing director of a trendy television channel.

Of course, being young and successful is fine—as long as you abuse it.

Years ago it used to be much easier to destroy a golden career, you could simply go out shoplifting. These days it's not enough, because everybody shoplifts, I know I do. Still, I bet Michael Jackson regrets not going for the old meat pasty-down-the-trousers routine, eh?

Successful women in their twenties and thirties can behave badly using sexual means; there have been several incidents in the media where, allegedly, well respected TV personalities have been heard via their radio mics to be having furtive sex with various crew members. One such woman who looks, on the surface, to be a bit of a tight arse, was overheard demanding to be fucked till she farted. That made me laugh a great deal and I'm only sorry that I can't tell you who she is.

45

BEHAVING BADLY IN THE WORKPLACE

(SOME JOBS HAVE BETTER PERKS)

THE ONLY POINT in having a job is to be able to steal from the workplace. This can range from the petty pilfering of toilet rolls to full-scale embezzlement. Some places are better to work in than others because the pickings are better. For instance, it is better to work in a biscuit factory than in one which manufactures light bulbs because eating broken biscuits does not make blood gush out of your throat. Equally, some jobs are better than others. The best jobs pay obscene amounts of cash and allow you to throw your weight around, making other people really unhappy. So knitting Fair Isle jumpers on a freelance basis from your croft on Skye is a rubbish job and doesn't impress me. What's the point in having a job that doesn't enable you to make long-distance calls at someone else's expense?

WORKING AT HOME

IS POINTLESS because you end up talking to yourself and sitting in front of the fridge eating. Then you make some calls to people who are too busy too speak to you. So then you have some fags and some more food and then you go back to bed and cry because you're so miserable. And all this time you're using your own heating and lighting. Sorry, this is all getting a bit personal but before I got involved with writing this I used to have a life. I used to go out and see people, now I find it difficult to speak and there is a lot of custard down my front. I've decided that shutting myself off in order to do a book is a bit dull, though I've tried to liven up the proceedings by stealing my own things and going into my study later and later, and telling myself off and making up excuses and then poking myself in the eye with a Biro. At the moment I'm taking myself to an industrial tribunal, accusing myself of sexual harassment (basically I'd rather have a wank than go to work, any day).

Before I made a career in stand-up comedy, the only other job I ever had was waitressing. I was a terrible waitress because I was a snivellingly anorexic and despised people who ate. So I'd gob in their food and hide a tuft of underarm hair in the potato, then chuck it down on the table and stand by making them feel guilty by murmuring things like 'you out-of-control pig person, stuffing your fat face just so it can come out as shit'.

BEHAVING BADLY IN PUBLIC

OUT AND ABOUT (SETTING AN EXAMPLE)

For some reason it is still more noticeable when a woman behaves badly in public than when a man does. This is why I am on a crusade of bad behaviour. Only when the standards of female etiquette are substantially lowered will we have true equality. If this means more women pissing on the street, then so be it.

BEHAVING BADLY IN AN ART GALLERY

Because everyone else is going round on tip toe, whispering, all you have to do is talk really loudly and you'll piss people off. However, just stamping around, yelling about your vaginal irritation is a bit easy. I suggest you visit a gallery when you're in a really bad temper because I find that when I'm furious, slashing the nation's heritage

with a Stanley knife makes me feel much better. To avoid being done for vandalism, remember you're making a statement – make sure you have a valid argument to justify your actions. If, for example, you've gashed a Rubens, tell everyone it's because you've had a pathological fear of fat women ever since Clare Rayner trod on your toe.

You can also pretend to be 'moved'; throw yourself in front of a Monet and sob. With any luck, some good-looking arty type will find you desperately attractive in a sensitive, weedy kind of way, and will join you on the floor to consummate the meeting of kindred spirits and bring you to a noisy climax. There, it's not been a wasted afternoon after all.

Most art galleries have a gift shop where you can buy tasteful items so that when people come round to your house there's proof that you've been to an art gallery. Whenever I go into these 'gift' shops, I always ask if they have that poster with the girl bending over the tennis court who has forgotten to put her pants on, because I think it's a classic. Failing that, I normally ask for a postcard of that bird who looks a bit like Bo Derek coming out of the sea with her tits hanging out.

NATIONAL TRUST HOUSES

THE PEOPLE WHO work in National Trust houses have always got something wrong with their brain. They believe that they are the caretakers of something of monumental importance to the country, such as a house with no central heating. They think they're big, they get confused and end up thinking they're the toffs who live there, when in fact they live in small houses three miles away and have to cycle to work. IT IS YOUR JOB TO REMIND THEM OF THIS FACT. When visiting a stately home, try and take one of those kiddies who's been reared by wolves and let them run loose, up and down the curtains. If you get tired walking round somewhere posh, climb into one of those four-posters and have a snooze. Make sure you use the chamber pot, after all, it's not an ornament. These places pride themselves on being totally authentic, so creep in at the dead of night and install strip lighting.

IN THE CINEMA

Arrange to be heavily pregnant and give birth half way through the movie – that should create some interesting shadows on the screen. Compete with Arnie as to who can grunt the loudest, or even better, swear all the way through a Merchant-Ivory. Obviously, only going to the cinema when you are in the throes of labour cuts down on the number of movies you can get to see per annum, but hey! You can always get a video out. NB, remember to have the child adopted, you only did it to outshine Daniel Day-Lewis (no one's going to notice how brilliant he is at painting with his left foot while simultaneously doing a really good Irish accent when you're on the front row with your legs akimbo and loads of red stuff is spurting out).

If you can't be bothered to go through childbirth in order to irritate people in the cinema, there are lots of other things that you can do, like sit in the middle of a row and get up to go to the toilet every five minutes; take along some spare ribs to eat as noisily as possible; wear a big hat; mug the ice-cream girl; take some Japanese chums and translate very loudly, or just run naked round the auditorium and see how long it takes before anyone catches you.

IN POSH DESIGNER CLOTHES SHOPS

Go in with a couple of your fattest mates, spitting cake crumbs and demanding something in a size 16, preferably turquoise Crimplene. Notice the prices and start rolling round the floor laughing. The shop assistant will be too weak from hunger to do anything. Make sure you laugh so hard that snot comes out of your nose and lands on a gown which will later be sold to an unsuspecting Tania Bryer.

IN SHOE SHOPS

Ask if you may borrow a pop sock, but instead of putting it on your foot, place it over your head, nip out and rob a bank, return with the cash and buy as many shoes as you like, plus some you don't like, what the hell.

IN AN OXFAM SHOP

Ask if they have any heavily urine-stained trousers or ladies' bras that smell of BO When they say 'no', look very surprised and leave.

IN THE PUB

Pubs are great places to behave badly because you can buy alcohol in them and turn into an obnoxious twat. Well I do, anyway. The problems arise when you haven't got quite enough money to get pissed in the pub, but you have a raging thirst. When I was poor, I used to go in pubs, order a lime juice and water and then sit sipping my drink until, for no apparent reason, I would slide off my stool and lie on the floor, seemingly in a deep faint.

WAYS TO MISBEHAVE IN THE SWIMMING POOL

- DRINK ALL THE WATER

- TAKE A PIN WITH YOU AND DEFLATE CHILDREN'S ARMBANDS

- WEE WEE

- RELEASE YOUR TAMPON, LET IT FLOAT INTO THE ONCOMING PATH OF SOMEONE WHO SWIMS WITH THEIR MOUTH OPEN

- GO ON A LIFESAVING COURSE. WHEN THE INSTRUCTOR TELLS YOU TO DIVE FOR THE BRICK, MISHEAR AND DIVE FOR THE PRICK – ANY OLD TODGER WILL DO. THE RESULTING HIGH-PITCHED SQUEAL WILL ALERT PEOPLE TO THE POSSIBILITY OF THERE BEING A STRANDED WHALE IN THE POOL, CAUSING WIDESPREAD ALARM

- PRETEND TO HAVE CRAMP, AND FLAIL AROUND UNTIL YOU GET A SNOG OFF A DISHY LIFEGUARD

- DO A BELLY FLOP FROM THE TOP BOARD. WATCH THE WATER TURN RED

- SMOKE – DOING THE BACKSTROKE IS THE BEST WAY OF KEEPING YOUR FAG DRY

I don't know why, but if you faint in a pub, the landlord will start pouring brandy down your throat in an effort to revive you. So every Friday night I used to do a fainting circuit round the pubs in Greater Manchester. By the time I'd had eight, I was ready to hit the clubs. On my last faint, I would come round, only to find that some toe rag had taken advantage of my unconscious state to steal all the money out of my purse! (The crying bit was easy, brandy always makes me maudlin.) There'd be a big whip round and I'd collect about thirty quid to see myself 'home safely' or rather into the Hacienda with enough spare to buy some amphetamine sulphate. Tee hee.

But women, you know what it's like when you walk into the pub and you just fancy a quiet drink, and there's loads of beery blokes all huddled together watching the bloody match on the telly— and they don't even notice you! Well I won't stand for that kind of treatment, so I march right up to the telly and turn it off, only when they notice the fact that I am a woman and therefore require a certain number of ribald comments about my breasts will I leave them alone. Unless of course *Brookside* is on, in which case they can shut up or piss off.

The time to stop going to your local pub is when you walk in and you realise that you've slept with every bloke in the place and the little old guy with the limp and the metal plate in his head that collects the glasses gives you a look of confidant expectation.

DEPRESSION

This is often caused by not being able to give up things like booze, fags and mind-bending drugs. I suffer from the most terrible depressions. You know it's going to be a bad day when you wake up and the birds are singing Leonard Cohen numbers and you immediately start to question the meaning of life: war? Famine? What the fuck are you going to do with your hair? You know what it's like when you're on the verge of a depression, just one little thing will tip you over into the abyss, something like finding out that actually, Emma Thompson is a really nice person. All of a sudden you hate yourself more than rice pudding and you realise that you are snot on the sleeve of the universe. Listen, these aren't my words, this is my therapist speaking. She says to me, 'Yes, Jenny, you are a cunt, now give me £40 and fuck off, you're boring the tits off me.'

BEATING DEPRESSION

Twice, in the past I have been referred by my despairing GP to therapists. The first time I was faced with a woman who had extremely fat ankles, not helped by American tan tights and hideous plastic shoes. I spent all my sessions weeping. Not because of some hitherto unearthed childhood trauma, but because her legs depressed me. How could I trust this woman with my precious emotional baggage when it was blatantly obvious that she was so utterly hopeless, she couldn't even dress herself properly? My second experience with a shrink was much better. She was a very jolly lady who I first encountered falling over in the hospital car park. She went arse over tit, laddered her tights, smashed a bottle of Vimto and lay on her back calling Christ an abysmal piece of shit. We got on famously; at last, I thought I had found a woman who truly understood my psychosis. We were making great progress until it transpired that she wasn't actually qualified and had recently been sectioned under the Mental Health Act for impersonating a psychotherapist. She was bonkers. Maybe I should have guessed, but I thought the name Florence Nightingale was just a coincidence, and that wearing a crinoline was just a sensible way of disguising thick ankles.

I have given up on going to see people who are obsessed with the reason that you're feeling a bit low is because your father shagged you senseless. These days I find I can cheer myself up quite easily by going into a shop and spending a lot of money on leather items.

Jenny Eclair's Book Of Bad Behaviour

Some man called Rorschach or something decided that looking at ink blots could tell him whether you'd been Satanically abused. What do these ink blots look like to you?

(A. the top one is Marilyn Monroe, the bottom one is a daffodil)

THE PHYSICAL PAIN OF BAD BEHAVIOUR

BROKEN LIMBS

Limbs are frequently broken as a result of behaving badly. You might, for example, be climbing up a tree in pursuit of that rare bird's egg, when the bough breaks and you come crashing down, breaking a femur or collar bone. Or you may be in the pub and a fight breaks out. Because you are a bloody nuisance, you will not be able to resist joining in, even if it has nothing whatsoever to do with you. In the process, you will get a thorough thrashing from both parties, who resent your interference.

Getting drunk will often lead to the fracture of some part of your anatomy because you start thinking you are capable of super-human feats such as balancing on parapets 130 feet above concrete. I have never actually broken anything, but this is only because I am an incredibly supple drunk.

BAD BREATH

Due to smoking and drinking and eating kebabs. It is exacerbated by not cleaning your teeth until they are thick with a cheese-like coating, which means you can't close your mouth properly and as a result you cannot stop dribbling. That's what I find, anyway. People are very paranoid about having bad breath because in some instances it can smell like dog shit, which makes people suspicious of your diet. People who think they have bad breath eat lots of extra-strong mints, which are very bad for your teeth and cause dental decay, which is really whiffy. Aging school teachers always have halitosis. This is because in today's modern, trendy, liberal schools, teachers are not allowed to give the children the beatings they deserve and so have taken to breathing in their faces as an alternative form of punishment. Let me tell you, a face-to-face heavy-breathing confrontation with my old maths teacher Mr Shaw bought tears to my eyes far quicker than any amount of backside beating with a poxy slipper.

GANGRENE

People are always developing gangrene after walking across the North Pole in their pumps. They do this in order to donate money to their local hospital, which in turn has to fork out billions in saving the charity walker's toes, which have turned into little black stumps. It doesn't make sense.

However, there are easier ways of getting gangrene; dodgy body piercing is the easiest. Recently I decided to have my nipples pierced because I was sick of losing my car keys. I went along to the jewellery counter at John Lewis, got my breasts out for them to pierce and they went all funny on me! So I had to do it at home with a cork and a needle. I am very proud of the results apart from the fact that my right nipple is enormously elongated from shoving the key into the ignition.

PREGNANCY AND CHILDBIRTH

REASONS TO AVOID IT

YOU CAN NEVER GET A TAXI IF YOU ARE PREGNANT, BECAUSE CAB DRIVERS ARE PHOBIC ABOUT YOU GIVING BIRTH ON THE BACK SEAT (HAPPENS ALL THE TIME, ASHTRAYS FULL OF PLACENTA)

OF COURSE, the placenta is very useful, because it is so very hideous that by comparison, the baby is quite attractive – so you decide to keep it.

Another thing you should keep is the umbilical cord because at a later date you can attach mittens to either end.

When the umbilical cord is cut, it is tied into a knot; otherwise the baby would unravel. After a while this knot drops off. It's just a bit of blood and gut and skin, so I saved my daughter's. I thought it would be nice to put it on top of the cake at her eighteenth birthday. So I kept it in a matchbox on the mantelpiece. Unfortunately, some months later, I came home a bit pissed and smoked it.

YOU CAN'T DRINK AND YOU CAN'T SMOKE BECAUSE IF YOU DO, YOU WILL RETARD THE BABY'S GROWTH

(**THIS IS A BLOODY** good idea actually, because then it'll just drop out really easily and you can dress it in a sock.) I had a seven-and-a-half pounder—that's including the sesame bun, the relish and the pickled gherkin.

IT HURTS

Do you know, the bit that really hurt me when giving birth was when the midwife referred to my vagina as the birth canal – CANAL! It wasn't that big. Well, it wasn't until the baby pushed her great fat head down it. Now it's gone all baggy round the neck like a badly washed jumper. I don't use tampons any more, I just roll up a duvet, although they're a bugger to flush away.

STRESS INCONTINENCE

Otherwise known as 'pissing yourself', this is the result of not bothering to do your pelvic floor exercises after you've had a baby. Basically, it means that every time I sneeze I wet my pants.

Lots of people have asked me whether I am going to have any more children. NO. The only point in having more kids is if they can sing close harmony, then you can make some money out of them. Then again, remember the Nolan Sisters? Tie my tubes!

53

CONTRACEPTION

(SOME PEOPLE JUST USE THEIR PERSONALITY)

CONTRACEPTION is vital if you want to avoid having babies, and avoiding having babies is vital if you want to keep your vagina in the shape in which it was originally intended to be. After I had my daughter, I was very badly stitched by a left-handed doctor, so my fanny was as untidy as a bit of six-year-old's knitting – it was all tight in one place and then all loose in others. Something drastic had to be done. I was referred to a clinic that specialised in a revolutionary new method of dealing with this kind of problem. The clinic was so brand new that I was its first patient. I lay back with my knickers off and legs akimbo, while electrical currents were passed through a water-filled plastic bag strategically placed over my fanny. All of a sudden I became aware of noises in the corridor – it was a posse of dignitaries who'd come to declare the clinic officially open, headed by a politician. On opening the door of my cubicle they saw more than they had bargained for. The politician only marginally more embarrassed than when he fell into the sea during a photo opportunity. I thought it was very funny, and laughed so hard that all my stitches flew out and we had to start again.

THE PILL
A great invention which allowed you to shag around without getting pregnant. Then AIDS had to come along and spoil everything. Women who don't want to have sex because they have a headache are probably on the pill, because headaches are a common side-effect, which defeats the whole object, really.

THE CONDOM
Fine, unless it's got a whopping great hole in it, as I found out, to my cost.

THE FEMALE CONDOM (OR WINDSOCK) I once threw one of these out of the window and it got caught in a cross-wind and ended up in New York. Can also be used in place of a Sainsbury's carrier bag and vice versa.

THE SPONGE
I gave up on this one. I now use it to apply a nice even coat of foundation.

THE CAP
Fine if it's in the right place, which is over the cervix and not in the bathroom cabinet. Useful for indoor frisbee games.

THE COIL
My fave. I've got a Copper 7, so with any luck I won't be getting arthritis of the vagina, although I think I'm getting big green concentric circles all the way up. Imagine this coil inside, like a great big Slinky. You should see the way I come downstairs in the morning.

GAFFA TAPE
A very cheap method.

BEHAVING BADLY AT WEDDINGS

THE ONLY REASON to get married is to make all your best mates look really shit as bridesmaids. 'I don't care if you're 36, if I say Little Bo Peep crinolines and crooks, you fucking well do it, alright, bitch?' I have never been married. Once I was on my way to the church and I don't know what came over me, but I ended up having sex with the chauffeur of the limo. My poor father didn't know where to look. I have nightmares about getting married: there's one recurring dream where I'm walking up the aisle in a white frock, and I come on. By the time I get to the altar I'm having to hold my bouquet strategically over the rapidly emerging crimson stain, while whispering 'Have you got 10 pence for the Tampax machine?' to the vicar.

I do believe in marriages of convenience. Because I'm so shit at organising my own life I'd like a wife, something out of the *Stepford Wives* would do me. Something with a proper hairdo, who could fix me a martini at the end of the day and give me a blow job. Oh no, I'm getting confused that wouldn't work would it? Alright, I'd like to marry a nice domesticated homosexual with a fetish for wiping down formica and different vacuum-cleaner attachments. Preferably one who could give a good shoulder rub and has an American passport. Is that so much to ask? Let's face it I'd rather have access to a Green Card than a poxy food processor.

Aren't wedding-present lists tedious? When I get invited to a wedding I always give the newly weds a £50 voucher for a firm of solicitors that I know, so handy for when they decide to separate. Actually, I do get invited to a lot of weddings, and whenever I go, I throw rice, though I don't always take it out of the tin. I've got a dyslexic friend, and she throws mice.

In the past, I have often been invited to ex-boyfriends' weddings. Actually that's a lie, I'm not invited but I get to hear about them and I turn up, arriving several minutes after the bride wearing a spectacular wedding gown vastly superior to the one she's wearing. Then I position myself at the back of the church and wail. After the ceremony I like to get in on the photos, secure in the knowledge that I look more radiant than she does. I don't know about you, but malicious acts of spite always make my eyes sparkle.

CUT OUT AND KEEP

THE SPEECHES

THERE ARE LOTS of little pamphlets available to advise you on making a suitable speech, but cast these aside, trawl through the bride's murky past, remind the guests of what a little scrubber she used to be and how she might look as though butter wouldn't melt in her mouth, but everyone knows she's a **WHORE**. Brides' mothers always cry at their daughters' weddings, so make sure she's got a reason. Here's a best man's speech to cut out and use.

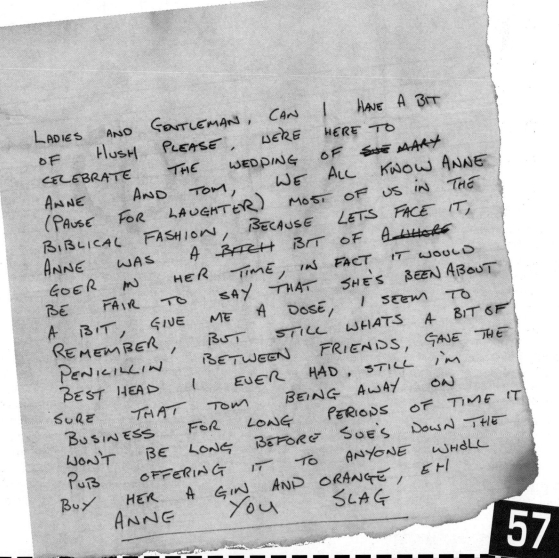

LADIES AND GENTLEMAN, CAN I HAVE A BIT
OF HUSH PLEASE, WERE HERE TO
CELEBRATE THE WEDDING OF ~~SUE MARY~~
ANNE AND TOM, WE ALL KNOW ANNE
(PAUSE FOR LAUGHTER) MOST OF US IN THE
BIBLICAL FASHION, BECAUSE LETS FACE IT,
ANNE WAS A ~~BITCH~~ BIT OF ~~A WHORE~~
GOER IN HER TIME, IN FACT IT WOULD
BE FAIR TO SAY THAT SHE'S BEEN ABOUT
A BIT, GIVE ME A DOSE, I SEEM TO
REMEMBER, BUT STILL WHATS A BIT OF
PENICILLIN BETWEEN FRIENDS, GAVE THE
BEST HEAD I EVER HAD, STILL I'M
SURE THAT TOM BEING AWAY ON
BUSINESS FOR LONG PERIODS OF TIME IT
WON'T BE LONG BEFORE SUE'S DOWN THE
PUB OFFERING IT TO ANYONE WHOLL
BUY HER A GIN AND ORANGE, EH
ANNE YOU SLAG

THE HEN NIGHT

SHOULD BE held sufficiently in advance of the wedding to allow for complete recovery following a liver transplant. The bride to be must be taken out on the town by a gang of women who know how to breach the peace professionally. The evening's entertainment must consist of the following: getting pissed, shoving the bride-to-be's face into the male stripper's jock strap, a cat fight, some tears, some broken nail extensions, the wetting of panties from laughing and crying at the same time, the inhalation of vomit and mouth-to-mouth resuscitation.

THE STAG NIGHT

SHOULD BE held sufficiently in advance of the wedding to allow for any prison sentences that might have to be served as a result of pissing in public places, exposing genitalia, punching coppers, and so on. Stag nights have a habit of ending up in tears and are quite frequently the 'cause of death' on a coroner's certificate. The saddest ad I ever read in *Exchange & Mart* read: 'For sale, one size 12 Pronuptia wedding dress, never worn, would swap for outfit suitable for a funeral.' That's the selfishness of men. After all the time and trouble Aunty Jean went to icing the cake, and what with the expense of the bridesmaids' dresses and the car hire, you'd think the bastard would have the decency not to fall stark bollock naked off the midnight express to Hollyhead.

Men who manage to survive their stag night spend the next six weeks in a lather of nerves, constantly checking their penis for any yellow discharge that might be the result of sleeping with that syph-riddled prostitute his mates set him up with.

THE WEDDING RECEPTION

I ONCE WENT to a spectacularly rough wedding in South-east London. The 'breakfast' consisted of a trestle table groaning with whelks (possibly because they were still alive). The blushing bride – so called because she was in the toilets going down on the best man when the speeches were being made – caused her new husband such embarrassment that the only thing he could do was fight with everyone. In the ensuing rumble, the bride's pearls were broken and scattered all over the place, resulting in many old folk skidding and breaking their hips. Eventually things calmed down and in customary Lewisham tradition, all the guests were invited to shove five-pound notes into the bride's garter as a sort of honeymoon send-off thing. Unfortunately, this particular bride never made it to her honeymoon, because with £600 stuffed up her garter, and what with this being South London, she was mugged on her way to the car – by her father, which was a bit embarrassing.

THE BRIDE

SHOULD HAVE LOST an enormous amount of weight so that she can squeeze into a frock so tight it damages her internal organs. During the reception she should get a bit pissed and start scoffing everything in sight until some seams burst. She will have had her hair and make-up done by a professional who specialises in making all brides look like the girl who came sixth in the Miss Blackpool Pageant back in 1973. When she watches the video of the event she will be able to hear her friends bitching about how awful she looks. Videos are a big mistake at weddings. At my cousin Jonathan's, I feature very prominently, loudly congratulating his bide Dianne as she emerged from the church. This would have been fine if my cousin had married Dianne, who was his old girlfriend, but he'd just got himself hitched to a Zoë. She should have been wearing her name badge from the supermarket where she works. That wedding video is a constant source of embarrassment, especially the bit in which my sister and I pretend to be Pepsi and Shirley singing old Wham numbers. I was so humiliated by this being on film that when Jonathan and Dianne – sorry, Zoe – were on their honeymoon, I broke into their house and stole it. Obviously I had to make the burglary look authentic, so I nicked their wedding presents as well.

THE BRIDESMAIDS

IT'S BEST IF there is a very fat bridesmaid with gland problems and a very thin bridesmaid with an eating disorder. There should also be a third bridesmaid who is very pretty, but a hopeless drug addict. I once attended a posh wedding where the bride's three sisters were all coke-heads; they zoomed down the aisle wired off their tits, chewing gum, and sniffed furiously during the prayers. Unfortunately, one of them was a hayfever sufferer and as she walked out of the church she sneezed so violently that what was left of her nasal passages sprayed out over the radiant bride, who looked like she'd been rolling around in an abattoir.

THE MOTHER OF THE BRIDE

LOTS OF BRIDES' mothers spend the months leading up to the wedding suffering from a mystery illness and no longer have the use of their legs. They always determine, however, that come the day they will walk down the aisle. This they do, with lots of face-pulling and grunting noises. So many women cannot bear the thought of their daughter having all the attention, even for one day.

THE FATHER OF THE BRIDE

EASY TO SPOT, he's the one with the hunted look in his eye, the one who forked out for all this, and if he had his time again he'd marry a Muslim because they tend to abort baby girls. Later he will get so pissed that he will sexually molest the fat bridesmaid on the grounds that she's so fat she should be grateful.

THE HONEYMOON

THE GOOD THING about booking into a hotel as a honeymoon couple is that you tend to get a complimentary bottle of champagne. I often pose with my boyfriend as a pair of newly weds: all it takes is a bit of confetti around the shoulders and a horrible going-away suit; best suite in the hotel, magnum of bubbly. Then we bounce around on the bed making farmyard noises as if we aren't really bored stupid with each other and still have sex. We leave in the morning looking embarrassed and sheepish and they think it's because they've overheard us having sex, when in fact it's because we've stolen their towels, light fittings and decorative display of dried flowers.

THE WEDDING DJ

MUST HAVE A crap system, must wear a novelty bow tie and encourage people to play games, the first person to bring him a pair of ladies' knickers wins a prize (this backfired on the DJ at a recent wedding I attended, because I decided to wrestle the bloomers off an elderly female relative who suffered from dual incontinence).

THE BOUQUET

TRADITIONALLY SHOULD be thrown at a load of spinsters. This can have disastrous consequences if it's made up of cacti.

THE UPPER MIDDLE CLASSES

C an't actually bear the thought of not being upper class, so in a bid to rise above their station, they behave very badly indeed. But they can't afford to do it properly and bankrupt themselves by having to 'start again'.

The upper-middle classes have lots of opportunities to get extremely pissed in the name of being sociable. Inevitably, this means they get their secretary pregnant, lose their driving licence, their job, wife, kids and home, so end up living by themselves in rented accommodation. Serves them right, doesn't it?

The upper-middle classes like uniforms and dressing up – they wear old minor-public-school ties and – more often than not – ladies' underwear.

Upper-middle-class women always have that hunted look of someone who has drunk too much sherry to do the school run. They are often very bitter because they've been left for a younger woman. Their lives are full of broken-down washing machines, which they break on purpose in the hope that a dishy young labourer will come by and give them a good servicing. They are usually very highly strung and suffer from such emotional problems as nymphomania. They are desperate to shag anything, particularly since they have had a tummy tuck. Their favourite occupation is being caught in their Janet Reger underwear by the man who's come to clean the pool. They are willing to fork out pots of money on tennis gear in the hope that they'll get off with the coach. They make a point of only ever employing male au pairs.

The upper-middle classes are never satisfied – they always take things back to shops and demand to have the sales assistant beaten. This is because they're really into corporal punishment. For example, the women will spend a lot of time pummelling their thighs under the pretext of getting rid of cellulite, when in reality, they just enjoy it.

Upper-middle-class men believe in discipline to the extent that they beat their children with wooden spoons and then get all confused when they get an erection.

Upper-middle-class children get expelled from school for trading their mothers' barbiturates in the playground. They absolutely despise their parents and rebel as soon as they can by joining a hippy commune and never changing their jeans.

The final act of revenge by upper-middle-class children is to bring a mixed-race grandchild home and stand well back while their parents thrash around on the carpet.

HOLIDAYS

HOLIDAYS

HOLIDAYS ABROAD

The thing about going abroad, is that foreign countries have quaint little customs, and the natives get all peevish if you enter their churches improperly dressed. I have learned by experience that it's better to put your bikini top back on before you enter a religious building. Anyway, it's safer not to be topless when you light candles. I was in Rome once and failed to cover my breasts adequately. The pain of dripping hot wax on my tits was exquisite, but people tend to get a bit funny about you having noisy orgasms in the Vatican. Guide books often warn British tourists that many people believe British women are loose and are therefore fair game for any local men. The books explain that we are liable to be continually pestered by swarthy types, but let's face it, why else do we go on holiday? I am always rather disappointed if, at the end of a day trawling around some ancient Muslim town, my arse isn't black and blue from being grabbed.

Some people spend a lot of time comparing sun tans, but I'm forever hoiking down my bikini bottoms to proudly demonstrate my pinch marks.

When choosing a holiday destination, I like to opt for a place where, physically, I'm at an advantage. Being blonde, I go to places that are swarming with dumpy, dark hirsute types, so by contrast, I will stand out as a thing of rare beauty. Basically, I like to be surrounded by hideous old boilers while I'm on my hols. I can't stand the competition in places like Cannes, which is full of people who look like the cast of *Bay Watch* just hanging out (mostly over their bikini tops). I also choose my holiday companions with care – it's pointless going away with someone who's going to look better than you on a beach, it will only depress you. On the other hand, it's a mistake to go with anyone who is so freakishly fat that its impossible to get a tan thanks to her torso casting a shadow the size of Crete.

I like to go away with someone who's just a bit mousey, next to whom I sparkle. My companion must also be accommodating and quite happy to vacate the shared bedroom and sleep on the balcony should I get lucky and score.

HOLIDAY ROMANCES

In the past I have been too keen, but now I try to hold back until I'm at least out of the airport. Getting off with a baggage handler is a tad desperate.

The Spanish waiter syndrome is another cliché to avoid: it is downwardly mobile shagging. Go for the hotel proprietor instead. I was once completely blinded by the owner of a Greek hotel. It wasn't love, it was the fact that he had a gob full of gold teeth and he owned every pedalo in sight.

Many older, recently divorced, women go on holiday in the hope of finding a little romance (in other words, a legover with a bloke young enough to make people laugh and point). These women often have a tragic habit of bringing their beach Lothario home with them, at which point Pedro instantly falls for his lover's daughter causing a family rift that will never be healed. Going out with a foreign type is good because it relieves the tedium of the British 'new man', who would never dare tell you what to do, what to wear, where to go, and, as we all know, is incapable of a decent shag.

Alarm bells should start ringing, however, when Johnny Turk confiscates your make-up bag, wraps you up in a big sheet and demands that you wear a veil. Never go out with someone who expects you to walk three paces behind them. Oh yeah, and remember, some of these people still wipe their arse with their hand. A futher word of advice: be wary of relationships that are based upon the fact that he looks cute in his beach thong.

At some point, he's going to have to put some clothes on. So just make sure you check

out his wardrobe. A friend of mine didn't. On the day she married Jesus, he was wearing a white nylon *Saturday Night Fever*-style suit and mock-croc slip-ons. That night she tore his clothes off him. In the hope that they'd be beyond repair.

LOOKING GOOD ON HOLIDAY

PEOPLE HAVE A HABIT OF GOING A BIT MENTAL when it comes to holiday clothes. All the fashion glossies advise lots of navy and white, which you can mix and match and look a bit nautical. Bollocks! We want ra-ra skirts and T-shirts which say 'Fuck me till I fart' on the front.

You can always spot a British guy on the beach, not only by his poor physique and the acne scars on his back, but by his comedy swimming trunks. We are a nation of arseholes and any attempt to pretend otherwise is a waste of time, but at least our men don't wear bracelets and carry handbags – not unless they're queer, that is.

The British do not have a clue about fashion. We also have really horrible bodies, and because they are always hidden under layers of tweed and big baggy jumpers from Marks & Spencer, we never really get to see them. This is why they are a bit of a shock to come across each summer, when we remove our protective winter coat of goose grease and venture out on to the beach, which is full of continental types playing frisbee, who are all bronzed and confidant, smug in the knowledge that they have superior skin pigmentation. Most British people are at a genetic disadvantage when it comes to looking good on the beach, and some of the really unlucky ones even have red hair and freckles.

These are commonly known as 'gingers', and are the butt of many a mean joke, all unfortunately compounded by the infamous Fergie sunbathing snaps, which proved that

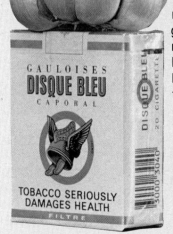

no matter how rich you are, if you have white skin and red hair you should wear a floor-length towelling robe and sit under a parasol. The only way these types are ever going to look tanned is if they sprout several more thousand freckles which miraculously join up. The other solution is to refuse anti-malaria tablets in the hope that you'll catch a minor dose and turn that funny yellow which, from a distance, could be mistaken for a lovely sun-kissed golden glow.

Personally, there is no point in me wearing a bikini, as the only thing I have to put in the top half is my picnic lunch. Instead I favour the one piece. My favourite has a polo neck and long sleeves.

I don't know what it is about going abroad, but for some reason you will be tempted to buy local fashion items. In Italy, for example, the women tend to get away with really slaggy clothes; lots of gold leather and satin appliquéd jumpers. I once treated myself to a very expensive Italian outfit, but unfortunately, whenever I wore it, people mistook me for a prostitute. French people are supposedly very chic, but in my opinion, they're ever so slightly grubby. In fact, I find it quite easy to adopt the French look by simply not washing for several weeks, reeking of Gauloise and garlic and growing my under-arm hair until it reaches my waist. The German style, however, is much harder to achieve, because they don't have any. And as for the Spanish, the only stylish people I ever saw in Barcelona were the transvestites hanging around the port. In fact, by comparison, it's a bit of a myth that we Brits are badly dressed and the next time I go abroad, I shall be flaunting my BhS labels with pride.

30P

SHOPPING ABROAD

In a lot of foreign countries, bartering is de riguer. This is so that when you return from places such as Tunisia, armed with hideous stuffed camels and nasty brass ashtrays, you can save face by saying, 'Well, it only cost me thirty pence.' Quite frankly, this whole haggling nonsense was invented to try to make you forget that you are wasting precious beer money on utter crap. The trouble with shopping abroad is that you can never work the funny currency out, unless you are a very tedious person with a calculator, which, in my experience, means that you eat lobster every day until you realise that lunch has been costing you £60 rather than the sixpence you believed it was. Then you find you are stuck in a foreign country with no money, giving you the options of either going out whoring or sitting by the side of the road begging. Of course this depends on what sort of clothes you have packed. I find it useful to take begging clothes with me wherever I go, because I tend to make more money doing that than I do from selling my body.

FOOD

If you eat that foreign muck you are bound to get diarrhoea. I know this for a fact. Once, when I was coming home from Greece, I had the most dramatic squits, which was great, because I lost loads of weight, but the unfortunate part was being stopped in customs at Heathrow by an official who seemed convinced that I had cocaine in my knickers! As if I'd want to snort anything that was in my knickers – I'd have had to have scraped it off the skid marks. I explained this in great detail to the gentleman, but at the same time I was having to shout to make myself heard above the explosions emanating from my nether regions. However, I think he got the message because all of a sudden he threw up into a potted plant.

HOLIDAYS

TIPPING

What a ridiculous palava tipping causes, especially if it's plutonium and you're tipping it into a kiddies' playground. I resent the fact that you're supposed to pay twice for some service. Of course, it can be a little difficult, you know how proud these peasants can be. So I normally just pretend my purse has been stolen, allowing a hasty exit pretending to run after the thief. Thanks to the power of T.V. advertising I learned that it's good manners to tip your hotel maid with some new form of sanitary protection. This works better if the maid is pre-menopausal. Although I once offered a withered little old raisin a press-on towel and to my surprise she held out for two. It turned out her shoes were a little too big for her.

A small sexual favour usually does it for male maids

SOME TIPS FOR YOU

Never trust foreign plumbing. The toilets, if there are any, never work properly. In places like Greece you are advised not to attempt to flush away your soiled loo paper, you're meant to just chuck it in the bin. Unfortunately where I was staying the bin was in the kitchen. After a couple of days there were flies everywhere and the whiff of old poo quite put me off my breakfast egg.

These days bidets are quite common-place, and we all know what to do with them. However, recently in Tunisia I was faced with a piece of bathroom equipment that I'd never encountered before. It consisted of a sort of stand-pipe thing coming out of the wall attached to a flexible hose with a nozzle on the end. When you turned it on water jetted out. I pondered for a while until I came to the conclusion that it was a D.I.Y. bowel irrigation device. Days later I was informed that it was in fact something to wash sandy footprints off the tiled floor, but by then it was too late.

Another word of warning; watch what you say. It's very easy to offend Foreign types, so never be lulled into thinking that they can't speak English. Also remember that in Arab countries, if you admire their possessions, they feel duty bound to give them to you. Make sure you enthuse over the Rolls Royce and not the camel.

WHENEVER I GO AWAY I ALWAYS LIKE TO BRING A LITTLE MOMENTO BACK WITH ME, NORMALLY IT'S SOMETHING I'VE FILTCHED FROM THE HOTEL, FOR EXAMPLE I HAVE A VERY FINE COLLECTION OF MINI BARS FROM ALL AROUND THE WORLD. HOWEVER MOST SOUVENIRS ARE RUBBISH AND ONLY VERY COMMON PEOPLE BUY THEM. I TEND TO WAIT UNTILL I'M BACK AT HEATHROW THEN I NIP INTO KNICKERBOX AND TRY AND BARTER FOR SOME PANTIES, INEVITABLY THE POLICE ARE CALLED WHICH IS VERY USEFUL BECAUSE IT MEANS BEING DRIVEN HOME IN A POLICE CAR, THUS SAVING ME THE CAB FARE ALL THE WAY BACK TO CAMBERWELL. LAST TIME THIS HAPPENED I WAS SO WORRIED ABOUT NOT HAVING PRESENTS TO TAKE HOME TO MY FRIENDS, I NICKED THE POLICE CAR RADIO AND AN OFFICERS HAT, NOT PARTICULARLY ETHNIC BUT GREATFULLY RECEIVED ANYWAY.

POSTCARDS SHOULD BE CHOSEN ON GROUNDS OF BAD TASTE, CAMEL WITH AN _ERECTION_ IS A GOOD ONE, SO IS ANYTHING THAT ATURES A GIRL WITH HER _TITS_ OUT, I HAVE TRIED TO FIND COMBINATION OF THE TWO SO FAR TO NO AVAIL, BUT MAYBE YOU KNOW A BOX NUMBER I CAN CONTACT!

Printed somewhere foreign

ALTERNATIVE HOLIDAYS

THE PACKAGE HOLIDAY

The cheap way of getting some sun; all you have to do is go somewhere hot and sunny and as long as you bring a package back, it won't cost you a penny. What drug running might cost you, of course, is your life. What a pisser eh? But you know what it's like - sometimes you'd give anything to be sitting in the sun, even if it means swallowing dozens of condoms stuffed with heroin. And let's face it, we're all used to swallowing stuff we don't like, aren't we girls? Obviously this kind of holiday has an even higher chance than most of ending in tears. Just when you're thinking, 'Oh great, this time tomorrow I'll be at home watching

Eastenders', you're bending over and someone with large hands is checking out the contents of your buttocks. Next thing you know you're sitting on the floor of a prison in Thailand waiting to be hung. Just make sure you

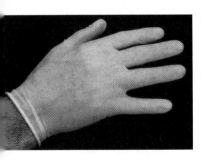

get someone to take a snap of you as you're taken away to be executed; everybody's got pics of themselves belly dancing or pretending to push the leaning Tower of Pisa over, you'll have something a bit different and you have to admit, until you've been sentenced to death thousands of miles from home, you've not really travelled, have you?

HOLIDAYS IN THIS COUNTRY

What an utter misery holidaying in this country is. I once went camping and after three hours I was so bored that I started sniffing butane gas from the industrial-sized canister on the campsite. Then I wrote a poem. Here is my ode to camping:

'TENTS NERVOUS HEADACHE'

The only good thing about tents is that they are very easy to rob. Unfortunately the pickings tend to be a bit crap, because people don't take their tiaras on camping holidays. That's the problem with the whole set up, campsites are full of bearded types of both sexes wearing horrible clothes who have sing-songs around camp fires. Basically they deserve to have their radios stolen — and their homemade fruit cakes, and their spare bobble hats, and just one fell walking boot and their torch. Actually, stealing the next door campers' torch rather back fired on me, because when he needed to go for a dump in the middle of the night he couldn't see where he was doing it and filled my boyfriends' welly. Which served him right for taking me camping. The easiest way out of a camping holiday is to drive a tent peg through your foot. I'd rather be slightly crippled than sleep under canvas ever again.

WHEN WE WERE KIDS, my parents used to take me and my brother and sister caravanning. I'd forgotten about this until I did a regression work shop with my therapist. Apparently lots of my problems stem from hearing my parents having sex in that caravan.

Thinking about it now I feel a bit queasy. I'm sure they wouldn't have done it if the awfulness of caravanning hadn't turned them to drink. My mother used to begin the day by having vodka on her cornflakes. It was the only way she could get through the day, cooped up in that vile Sprite 400 while it pissed down with rain and us lot ripped each others' arms and legs off. The worst type of Caravanners are the professionals who belong to the Caravanning Club of Great Britain. These are the people who have all the kit; the awnings and swing ball and badminton nets and barbecues and pump action Uzi machine guns for when people accidentally tread over the invisible line that mark their territory. These people are very dangerous and I don't think it's sufficient that they should have a measly car sticker warning you who they are; they should be branded.

CARAVANNING CLUB OF GREAT BRITAIN

HOLIDAY CAMPS

NOT AS FASHIONABLE NOW. Not since the advent of Biosphere holidays, or Centre Parcs. Back in the '70's these were the places to go if you wanted to behave really badly. Really lucky people even got paid for committing acts of gross indecency. They were called **RED COATS** and were recognised by the fact that they were covered in old semen stains and smelt of stale sex. In holiday camps you were encouraged to behave appallingly under the guise of good old fashioned clean fun. For example, cash prizes could

HOLIDAYS

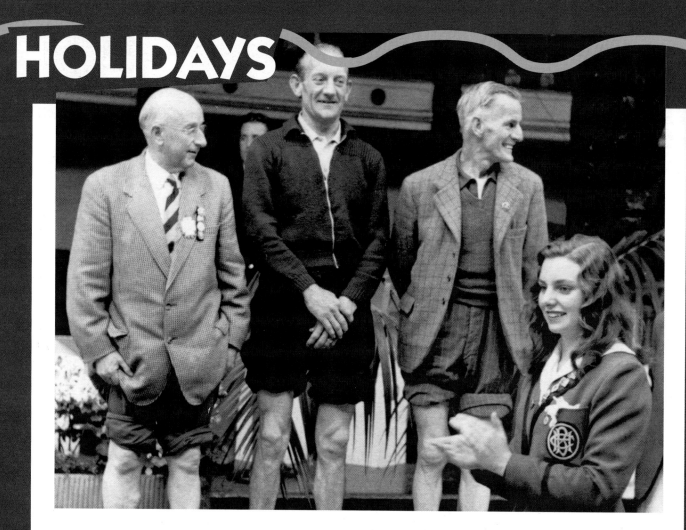

be won in the 'wartiest penis' and 'biggest Herpes' competitions. As a teenager living near Blackpool I was desperate to go to one, even if it was just for the day. But my mother wouldn't let me, and to this day she still doesn't know that every Saturday, when she thought I was doing odd jobs for a blind man round the corner, I was pinching money from his tea caddy and spending it on a day pass to paradise — or Pontins as it was better known. I do feel a bit guilty about that blind old man, but then I think, 'well, he couldn't see that I hadn't cleaned his flat'. And he must have been fond of me because when he died he left me the contents of his tea caddy. Which by that time amounted to 17p.

HIRING A COUNTRY COTTAGE

You flick through a brochure and choose a sweet, pretty cottage with a thatched roof and hollyhocks. Fill in a booking form, send off vast sums of money and get very excited. Then a letter from the hire company arrives two days before you're due to go; the cottage has burned to the ground, but they can offer you an alternative — a flat above the Gents that's so dingy you have to leave the light on all day even in July. The kitchen consists of a bottle opener and a candle which you end up incorporating into vicious sex games with the clients of the Gents because you're so bored. (Actually, this was the best holiday I ever had.)

THE MIDDLE . AGES

CRISIS TIME

MEN: grow your hair, even if you only have one strand, put it in a pony tail and insist that you are 23 again. Start dressing in a bizarre fashion; be a cowboy or a train driver or a doctor (score extra points if you manage to con your local hospital into letting you perform major surgery). Wear stacked heels (the fact that you're shrinking is your business). Use Ian McShane as your role model – young girls like that wizened imp look. Only go out with women half your age, dance like John Travolta. This is the time to be really selfish! Sell the golf clubs, get a surf board. Ditch the bi-focals and swap them for coloured contact lenses. Tell your boss to 'fuck off', cash in your pension, buy an E-Type, crash it into a tree, hit a copper and nick ladies' underwear off clotheslines. Do everything you've been dying to for years but were too chicken. Finally, when the money's run out and your hernia's flared up, the wife's suing you for maintenance you can do the honourable thing. Which is, of course, faking your own suicide.

> **IF YOU HAVE** spent all your life behaving yourself, now is the time to go mad. Blame it on the hormones. Start being an idiot and get divorced for no reason – reject all responsibility!

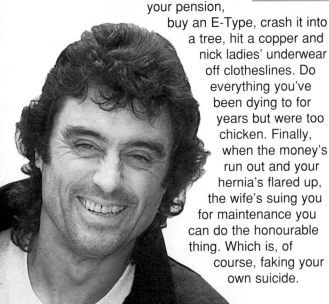

Middle-aged WOMEN should avoid HRT. Having a difficult menopause is the best excuse in the world to behave absolutely appallingly. I used to think most big supermarkets had something in their public-relations manifesto that advised staff to be lenient towards menopausal shoplifters. This was because I was in my local supermarket when I saw a middle-aged woman blatantly shoving frozen dinners into her tights while the staff pretended not to notice. It turned out that the woman was in fact the store detective who'd been having a lot of hot flushes and vaginal dryness, so everyone was too frightened to approach her in case she went into one. Many women in their fifties find themselves at a bit of a loose end; the kids have left home, they've got a dishwasher – they've nothing to do. This is when experimenting with lesbianism comes in handy. A recent survey said four out of five women preferred it to cleaning out the airing cupboard. Another survey said four out of five women in this age bracket would rather clean out the airing cupboard than have sex with their husbands.Just because you're getting on you don't have to play bridge, you can set up a weird religious cult in your front room, entitling you to have sex with young boys. Make sure the *News of the World* gets to hear of your antics, with any luck they'll come round and take incongruous photos of you, flaunting your varicose veins in a skimpy black negligee,wearing that slightly dazed look of a woman who drinks in the morning.

BEING AN AGEING *Slag*

THERE IS ACTUALLY no age limit to being a slag, it just gets sadder as you get older, but with any luck you'll be so brain-damaged with syphilis, you won't care. Perhaps the time to stop showing your cleavage is when it becomes withered, like an ancient Cox's Orange Pippin, and is smothered in liver spots. I have never had a cleavage, but that doesn't stop me drawing one on in Biro.

The older slag's best friend is, of course, her make-up bag. This contains the real tricks of the trade – the wherewithal to make your face look twenty years younger than your neck. No self-respecting slag is ever seen without make-up, but the trouble is that it can come off (on bed linen in particular – true slags are never sober enough to cleanse and moisturise at the end of the day). To prevent make-up sliding off, liberally apply a coat of clear nail varnish over the top and then just watch out for chips in the veneer. I've discovered that natural light is best avoided. The meanest lyrics in the history of pop have to be from 'Maggie May': '*The morning sun, when it's in your face, really shows your age.*' Rod Stewart has never been a kind man to women over the age of twenty-three. To spare any humiliation, these days I sit, alluringly, in dark corners, madly sucking in my cheeks. The ability to lie convincingly about your age is necessary when trying to get off with younger men, because for some reason they can get a bit squeamish if they realise that you are biologically old enough to be their mother. Don't be caught out on the small details such as Chinese horoscopes and I would rather forgo two weeks in Bali than let him see my passport. Whatever you do, resist all temptation to convert today's prices back into old money. I remember when I was thirty (a year before I decided I wanted to be), my sister gave me a lot of crockery with my age and the date emblazoned all over it. Naturally I smashed it up. Similarly, you must systematically go through your record collection, ruthlessly destroying anything that might incriminate you.

To prolong successful whoring it is wise to avoid childbirth. Having babies gives you stretch marks. Mine are like tyre tracks (Pirelli actually want me for next year's calendar). However, accidents will happen, in which case, my advice is to beat into your offspring that they are, in fact, your siblings. Even better is if you can persuade their grandparents that this is the case and they can bring them up, leaving you free to go to the pub.

There is nothing more traumatic for the groovy thirtysomething than to have a moon-faced fourteen-year-old lumbering around after you, cramping your style, by saying things like, 'Mummy, isn't it time you came home now'.

Ageing slags must fight the ravages of time. It doesn't involve health and fitness (never do anything that requires the removal of your stilettos), it means cheating. It means liposuction and facelifts. Why go to the gym when you can relax unconscious under a skilled surgeon's knife? There is nothing wrong with cosmetic surgery unless it leaks or explodes, but it is, however, very pricey. Home surgery is therefore a sensible option for those on low incomes. A simple facelift can be achieved by piercing baggy cheeks with kirby grips, drawing the skin up tightly and securing discreetly behind the ears. A lot of air hostesses do this; that's why they never take their hats off and can't stop smiling.

A SLAG'S WARDROBE
(Should ideally be full of naked, tawny-skinned seventeen-year-olds hiding from your husband)

OTHER ITEMS INCLUDE...

Lots of things with buttons that come undone accidentally on purpose. Anything with a zip that goes all the way down to your navel. Items that look like underwear but aren't. Leather jeans that show the contours of your genitalia, even when they're hanging up. A short, purple suede skirt, even though you can't get the spunk stains out. Stacks of fake leopard skin, Lycra, satin and lurex; avoid anything in tweed or corduroy, you're a slag, not a Sunday school teacher. Remember, short, tight and slit. Shoes should be many and varied, but never forget the subtle message of the white stiletto: follow me, fuck me. Thigh-length boots or anything made out of rubber or PVC (they don't need washing, just sponge them with a little Dettol). A lot of men like the idea of grown women in school uniforms and I still have mine. It consists of yards of brown Crimplene, matching orthopaedic shoes and a bowler hat. Even sadder, my boyfriend likes it. I also have an adult sized Ninja Turtle outfit, just in case.

Slag
LINGERIE

PANTS SPLIT INTO TWO CATEGORIES: nice ones, and ones that look as though they've been exhumed from the corpse of someone who was frightened to death.

Wannabe sex kittens should really buy lingerie from a catalogue advertised at the back of a tabloid newspaper. Ideally, underwear should be red, run in the wash and cause genital irritation. Cotton pants are for sensible people, whereas experienced old slappers always have a tube of Canesten at the ready.

Brassieres are interesting. I spend a lot of time wondering what it would be like to have something to put in one. It's especially sexy to reveal a great deal of grubby bra strap, as it proves that other people can't keep their filthy paws off you. I have never found a bra to fit me, even those stockingette trainer bras used to crumple up on my chest. I used to have one with a picture of a train on each cup, but they'd concertina so badly that it looked as though there'd been a major derailment.

Actually I'm really glad I don't have a cleavage – it would be full of fag ash in no time.

Many women these days resort to the 'body', because a Lycra one-piece is a great deal more

(ALL MY PANTS ARE NOW CROTCHLESS DUE TO THE GUSSETS HAVING ROTTED AWAY)

appealing than a lot of corrugated loose flesh. The trick with a body is to redistribute the fat, pushing it up from the midriff and shoving it into the bra cups – hooray, big knockers!

One last thought on bodies: never unpop your poppers, because you'll never remember to pop them back up again, and there you are, out on that hot date with the tail ends of your body flapping about. This is fine if you've just put a clean body on, but otherwise the ends look as though they've been dipped in custard.

I'm a martyr to vaginal discharge. The stuff that comes out of my vagina; pineapple chunks, slices of banana – I'm a walking trifle.

Jenny Eclair's Book Of Bad Behaviour

THE FAKE TAN is a marvellous invention, particularly if you have massive wibbly wobbly white thighs. I suspect Judith Chalmers wears fake tan, but she overdoes it; she's completely orange. She looks as though she's been Tango'd, for heaven's sake. Used sparingly, fake tan will give you the confidence to go to bed with much younger, taut-buttocked, bronzed male beauties (pool attendants and ski instructors, for instance).

Unsuccessful applications of fake tan will give you the unfortunate appearance of looking as though you've rolled around in a vat of tandoori paste and then spent a few hours in a clay oven.

For added authenticity, I actually use fake peeling. I attach filo pastry loosely to my shoulders and then shake'n'flake. Public-spirited members of the fake-tan fan club might like to carry a small battery-operated hand hoover for picking up discarded epidermis from friends' sofas. I just eat it.

Fake tan is much healthier than sunbathing as it doesn't give you skin cancer and, more importantly, makes you look like a babe. I'm very worried about melanoma. I once had a real mole removed from underneath my breast (not one of those sweet little furry creatures with a little pink nose, but one of those nasty skin moles), because I got sick of my boyfriend playing with it for 45 minutes, thinking it was my nipple!

Another advantage of fake tan, is that while everyone else is on the beach trying to go brown, you're in the hotel shagging a waiter.

Slag COIFFEUR

A good slag will make an effort with her hair. This basically means back-combing. Back-combing is the only exercise I ever indulge in. I find it quite exhausting and consequently I am taking steroids. Natural hair is rubbish and so are proper hairdressers; they fanny around, rambling on about follicles and PH balances. We don't want beet root-conditioner, we want peroxide and preferably peroxide that has been tested on small furry animals. If it doesn't blind rabbits then it's not strong enough. Bleach is the only answer to all hair problems. Even if you're a natural blonde, dye it – there is nothing like sitting in the hairdresser's, reading back copies of *Bella*, to make you feel superior. I particularly enjoy uplifting articles with titles like 'I was born with club feet but now I disco dance for Sheffield'.

When I was a fledgling tart I went through the poodle perm and the Farrah Fawcett Major flicked wings, but for some reason my mother still thinks that plaits suit me best.

At the moment I am in bouffant mode, as I'm working on the principle of the bigger the hair, the smaller the hips look in comparison. Physics O-level was not wasted. Whatever the style, hair should be set with an industrial-strength hair lacquer, which will enable it to withstand nuclear fallout. Or a night out on the piss, back to his place, rampant sex and the cab journey home (the latter being the tallest order).

Jenny Eclair's Book Of Bad Behaviour

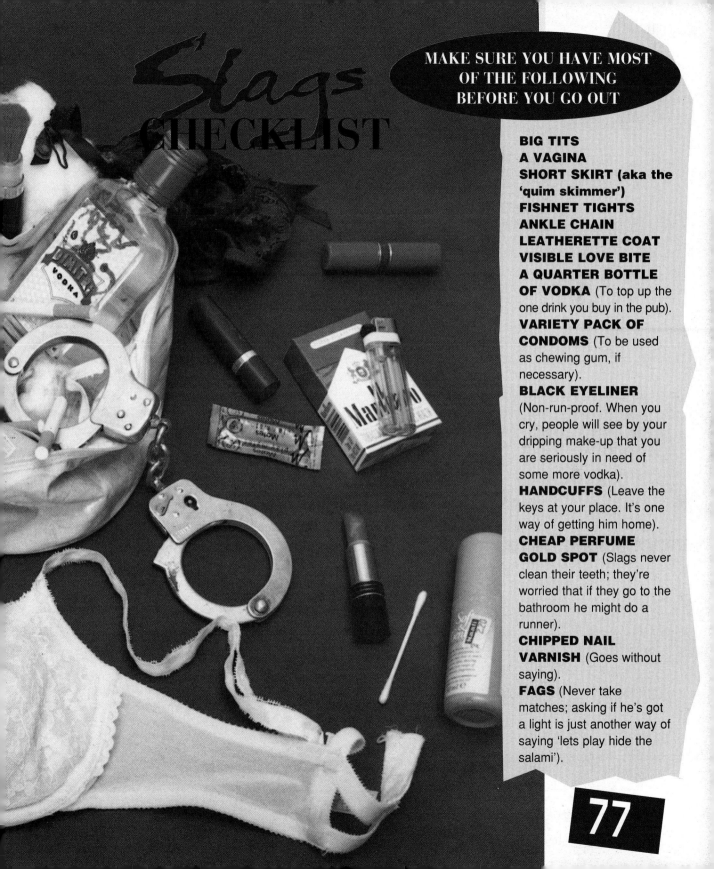

Slags CHECKLIST

BIG TITS

A VAGINA

SHORT SKIRT (aka the 'quim skimmer')

FISHNET TIGHTS

ANKLE CHAIN

LEATHERETTE COAT

VISIBLE LOVE BITE

A QUARTER BOTTLE OF VODKA (To top up the one drink you buy in the pub).

VARIETY PACK OF CONDOMS (To be used as chewing gum, if necessary).

BLACK EYELINER (Non-run-proof. When you cry, people will see by your dripping make-up that you are seriously in need of some more vodka).

HANDCUFFS (Leave the keys at your place. It's one way of getting him home).

CHEAP PERFUME GOLD SPOT (Slags never clean their teeth; they're worried that if they go to the bathroom he might do a runner).

CHIPPED NAIL VARNISH (Goes without saying).

FAGS (Never take matches; asking if he's got a light is just another way of saying 'lets play hide the salami').

77

WORKING
CLASS PEOPLE

I'm not talking your work-shy layabout here, I'm talking manual labourers and blue-collar workers. I'm talking salt-of-the-earth, down-to-earth types covered in soil or any kind of muck and oil and grease. Men in overalls with great big massive hands who get into fights and spend their entire pay packet on a Friday night. Real men who can't spell and are covered with tattoos. Men who eat with their hands and blow their noses really loudly, and spit phlegm impressively long distances. Real men who can fix your car and smoke roll-ups and look like Sean Bean... er, sorry, I'm just going to have a shower...

Working-class people are, of course, the scum of the earth. They are entirely irresponsible, with their cable TV and their children who play truant. They're the reason why this country's going to the dogs and its population eating convenience food. And they

generally have a better time than the rest of us.

They're like animals; great big, hairy, smelly animals, reeking of beer and belching in the face of society, in their soiled and sweaty vests, with their milk bottles on the table, generally lowering the tone.

And the women! The women! With their bosoms showing, and their bingo and their hen nights, clawing at male strippers, laughing, laughing at us, the tax payers! Flaunting themselves on the pages of porn magazines, cheating the DSS and dropping their 'h's and their skirts for any Tom, Dick – that's right, especially Dick – and buying gin instead of saving up for a conservatory. How dare they?

Jenny Eclair's

SLEEPING WITH THE WRONG PEOPLE

YOUR BEST FRIEND'S HUSBAND

This happens quite often on shared family holidays when, for some reason, you think it would be a good idea to rent a place in the sun with your closest chums.

Sun and sangria will inevitably lead to indiscretions and you will end up having stupidly loud sex with your pal's hubby. This, in turn, leads to a spectacularly stony silence at the breakfast table, I can tell you.

YOUR BOSS

Listen, he's the one with the expense account and the mobile phone. Sleep with him and you too can have these things. Or you tell his fiancée. Simple, really.

YOUR THERAPIST

All therapists are obsessed with sex. All they do is talk about sex, so you might as well do it. What else is the couch for? The best thing about screwing your therapist is that it makes them feel guilty and paranoid. Exploit this; spend hours talking about how having done it has led to all sorts of emotional trauma. Make up dreams that are easily analysed as being the result of abuse by a person in power, a person who will eventually pay you lots of money to go away.

MARRIED MEN

Married men are very nervous about scratch marks and love bites and lipstick on the shirt she bought him out of her housekeeping. Make sure you are very rough; pretend to be carried away with desire and send him out into the night bleeding. But don't overdo it. I once inflicted such a gouging and biting on a married man that he was able to go home and tell his wife that he'd been attacked by a wild cat. The wife immediately phoned the papers and the neighbourhood was instructed to keep an eye out for a stray puma. The married man had his photo in the local rag, his wife decided he was a hero and started giving him regular Wednesday-night blow jobs. All thanks to me. You see, affairs can save a marriage. Of course, married men are a bit dull. He is so racked with guilt that he forgets to enjoy the fact that he's paid for you to go to Paris with him, where you work your way through what would have been his children's' inheritance.

The trouble with married men is that they get ridiculously fat. This is because he will take you out for a clandestine lunch and then has to eat seconds of shepherds' pie when he gets home because it's his favourite. Eventually he will get so fat he will have a heart attack, so just make sure it takes place at his house.

I couldn't be bothered to have a serious

relationship with a married man because if he does leave his wife, she'll sting him for everything he's got and you'll end up looking after his teenage kids. You'll be really poor and all of a sudden you'll wonder what you ever saw in the fat, bald old git.

Basically, married men are lost causes unless of course they're...

POLITICIANS

Sleeping with politicians is a right laugh, especially the Tories, because they've all been to public school and are into really weird stuff. Obviously, it's hard to keep a straight face when you're tugging the minister's nipple clamps as hard as you can and he's wearing a nappy, demanding tinned rice pudding. I have no idea why so many right-wing ministers like bondage. Now, I'm not adverse to a bit of that myself, but as we know, it can go too far – all of a sudden you've lost the pulse and a simple act of making love has turned into one of necrophilia. What you're supposed to do at this point is get off and loosen the bonds, but hey, nothing's worth breaking a finger nail over, and it's one way of getting rid of this Government.

Jenny Eclair's

RELATIVES

Sleeping with any of your relatives really is a very silly thing to do as you will inevitably get pregnant and give birth to something that is physically hampered for life by its genetics: sticky-out ears and baldness are often the side effects of in-breeding (see the royal family). There are whole villages in certain parts of the country which are entirely populated by people with very short foreheads and exceptionally long middle toes, who are the result of cousins marrying. The advantages of having a relationship with a relative is that you already know his ghastly family, and it's not going to put you out of pocket more than usual at Christmas, considering you've been buying them a chocolate orange for as long as you can remember.

AXE MURDERERS (NEVER TRUST A MAN WHO SAYS 'DON'T STRUGGLE')

You know he's done time, but he's changed. This time it's different; he loves you, he's promised to give up drinking and going for long walks in the middle of the night. He wouldn't hurt a fly!

Go for it, but don't come running to me when an electric heater suddenly appears loosely screwed into the bathroom wall and he buys you comprehensive life insurance for your birthday.

BABYSITTERS

Come on, it's hardly your fault. Look at her – she's gagging for it. You're older, more mature, you've got grey slip-on shoes and your wife doesn't understand you.

You're under pressure, it's tough out there – the pressures of middle management are killing you and you're going bald into the bargain! And anyway, you've got to take her home, she can hardly walk the streets at night – anything might happen. So it might as well happen in your XR3i, all nice and cosy with Chris De Burgh on the stereo. She can't wait.

BEHAVING BADLY BETWEEN THE SHEETS

In my experience, a lot of men go all peevish when you take them to your bed and there's evidence of previous shenanigans all over the place. Giveaways include piles of used condoms quivering around like something out of a Stephen King novel, empty whipped-cream aerosols, and that sixteen-stone trucker from the night before still sleeping it off. This is very bad manners. Also, if there are any financial arrangements, make sure they don't come as a complete surprise. It's always so awkward after the event, having to tell people to their faces that there is no way they'd get a shag for nothing. Lack of communication in bed can lead to all kinds of disasters, for example a lot of people don't enjoy 'scatting' (dumping in their mouth) – it's all a question of taste. Farting in bed, on the other hand, is highly amusing. What you do is let rip with a really sloppy, boiled eggy kind of fart, then you trap your partner with the fart under the duvet until he's begging for mercy.

FAKING ORGASM (REALLY BADLY)

Say all the things he's desperate to hear, like, 'Wow, Baby, you're the best, I never got laid like that in my life. You're really something. Do it to me again big boy, fill me with your love muscle. Only say these things in a really sarcastic voice. He will never be sure of himself ever again. In fact, he will probably develop a stammer and start being very clumsy and get the sack from his job. Good, that'll teach him to be rubbish in bed.

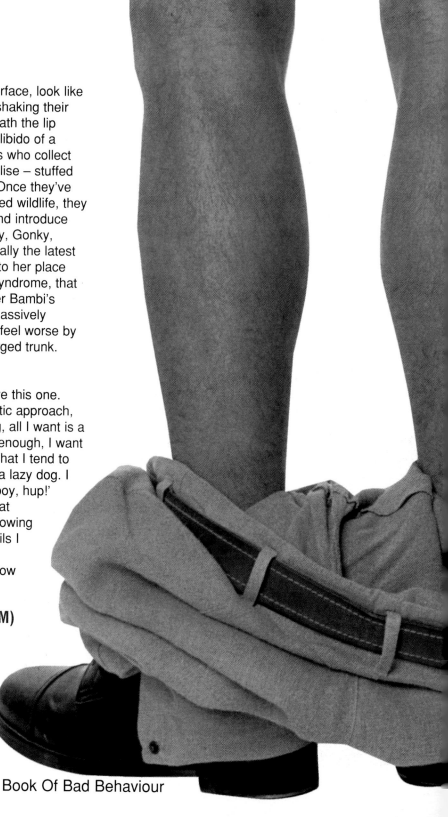

THE CUDDLY TOY SYNDROME

There are women, who, on the surface, look like really hot stuff. They're the ones shaking their tush in Stringfellows. But underneath the lip gloss and the Wonderbra lies the libido of a Giant Panda. These are the girlies who collect cuddly toys. Some of them specialise – stuffed owls being a particular favourite. Once they've got a complete menagerie of stuffed wildlife, they like to prop them up on the bed and introduce them: 'This is Fluffy, Bunny, Teddy, Gonky, Ducky and Floppy.' Floppy is actually the latest Spurs player who has gone back to her place only to fall foul of the cuddly-toy syndrome, that is, not being able to get it up under Bambi's reproachful glare. Meanwhile, a massively overstuffed Dumbo will make him feel worse by mocking him with his kapok-engorged trunk.

COPING WITH IMPOTENCE

All women's glossy magazines love this one. They always advise the sympathetic approach, saying stuff like, 'It's alright darling, all I want is a cuddle.' I say, 'No, this isn't good enough, I want a shag and I want a shag now.' What I tend to do is treat the reluctant penis like a lazy dog. I snap my fingers and shout, 'Hup boy, hup!' in a commanding sort of way. If that doesn't work, I encourage it by throwing chocolate drops at it, and if that fails I get the metal end of the lead and thrash it – basically, he's got to know who's boss.

BLOW JOBS (INC. FAKING THEM)

I do not give blow jobs. Why not? Because I find it really off-putting, seeing a grown man look that pathetically grateful. And anyway, you don't know how fattening it is. Of course, men really like blow jobs (another

Jenny Eclair's Book Of Bad Behaviour

reason not to give them). You know what it's like, there you are indulging in a bit of heavy petting, and all of a sudden you feel that pressure on the back of your neck and he's pushing your face down to his flies. OK girls, go with it. Go down on your knees, unzip, let the trousers drop and then just run for it – turn around and watch him do what I call 'the penguin' – waddle around with his trousers around his ankles saying, 'What's going on?'

CUNNILINGUS — WHAT IF HE'S NO GOOD?

Put him off, there is nothing worse than an amateur going down on you. The only people any good at cunnilingus are didgeridoo players because they can do circular breathing, which means they can go down on you for about six years. And that's how long it takes. Men are so clumsy. If you're fed up with him leaving your pubes full of chewing gum, put him off; wipe your bottom from back to front, or leave that tampon rotting in there for about six months. Well you did ask, didn't you? Oh no, you didn't?... Sorry.

DUMPING MEN AFTER A POOR PERFORMANCE (CRUEL BUT FAIR)

I normally award points for technique, artistic interpretation and originality. I often get my flatmate in to hold up score cards

(unfortunately

she's from East Germany and is very mean). If the man in question fails to live up to expectation, (he may lose points for things like expecting a cooked breakfast, or wearing nasty underpants) then I'm afraid he's out. I never say 'we can still be friends', because it's pointless having friends of the opposite sex who aren't capable of a decent shag when you're desperate.

BEHAVING BADLY WITHIN A SEXUAL RELATIONSHIP

OK, so you're going out with this guy. It's supposed to be a monogamous relationship built on trust. You trust him, he trusts you, he must be barmy. I recommend only having long-term relationships with men who don't wear lace-up shoes. That way you know they're too thick to realise that you are cuckolding them left, right and centre. To be habitually unfaithful, you just need the ability to lie and bluff your way out of potentially incriminating situations. For example, you come home from a Russian night class with your dress on inside out, knickers in your handbag, completely unable to speak Russian. What do you do? Answers on a postcard, please – I haven't got a clue. If I'd been able to get myself out of that one, I'd still be with Simon. Instead I was chucked out of the house and had to live in my car for three months.

Having an affair is exhausting. It's so easy for your partner to become suspicious. The antenna go up as soon as you start shaving your legs and worrying about dental hygiene and buying new panties. The only way is to become a complete slob so that no one in their right mind would want to shag you. Of course, promiscuity is not the only way to break up a stable relationship.

Other ways include 'fucking up the birthday present'. When it's her birthday, she will expect flowers and champagne and little sparkly things wrapped up in tissue paper. Buy her a bread bin. And when it's his birthday, forget it. He bought you a bread bin!

83

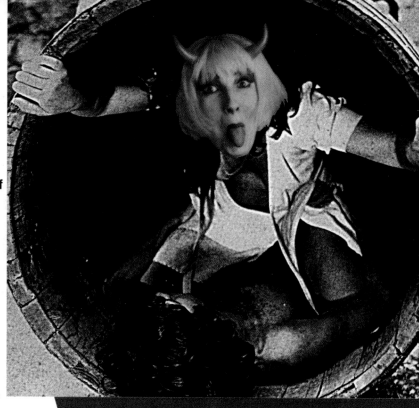

*i*t's impolite to have sex anywhere that is visible to other people who aren't having sex. Personally, I don't mind desperate couples taking advantage of a nice warm Tube carriage in which to copulate, especially if he looks like Sean Bean, as it saves on my video rental bill. What I can't stand are the sad cases that do it on their own. That really pisses me off, because I'm sick of getting out at Leicester Square with the back of my coat drenched in an anonymous donor's semen. So stop it, and you know who you are.

IMPOLITE PLACES IN WHICH TO HAVE SEXUAL INTERCOURSE

SUPERMARKETS
Great places to have a crafty whatsit, as the queues are often phenomenally long, especially on a Saturday. This means if you're clever you can get your boyfriend to stand close behind you and give you one. I don't know about you, but that piped music always turns me on. What's really nice is when the whole queue are doing it in one long chain and everyone comes together.

TELEPHONE BOXES
Used to be really good because you could drag him in, do the business and there was no possibility of him wanting to stay the night. The disadvantages were the stench of wee wee and people trying to get in to make calls. Of course, these days, telephone boxes are really rare, but often posh people have them in their gardens as ornaments, so that's worth checking out. But on the whole, boxes have been replaced by perspex hoods which might keep your hair dry while you're

bonking, but it means that your legs get very chilly, especially when your tights are down round your ankles.

IN YOUR PARENTS' BED
They really hate this, especially if they're trying to get some kip at the time.

ANTI-SOCIAL WAYS TO DISPOSE OF CONDOMS
Never forget that it is all too easy for small doggies to choke on carelessly discarded condoms. Just a thought...

Behaving badly in PUBLIC PLACES

CHURCHES

I once visited a Saxon Church in Little Snoring, a village without a pub in Norfolk. The churchyard was quite good because it was full of headstones bearing the tragic inscriptions of loads of babies and children who'd died in the great plague and I do like a good cry in a grave yard. Also, they're great places to pick up comedy names from the olden days which you can suggest to your friends when they have babies. For example, Arkwright Woodencock.

Inside the church, however, it was a bit dull apart from the visitors' book in which people had written things like, 'a spiritually uplifting place, may God bless this community'. Sandwiched in the middle of all this pious twaddle was the angrily scribbled comment 'boring as shit'. It was then that I recognised the writing and realised that I'd been there before.

AT THE THEATRE

Go and see *The Mousetrap* so that you can tell everyone whodunnit. This play has been running in the West End for 29 years, let's make this its last.

Heckling is character-building for any actor. Why should stand up comics get all the shit? It would do most members of the RSC good to be called wankers to their face. I bet they couldn't cope, I bet they'd just cry. Don't actors make you sick? They're always going on about what utter torment it is to act, when all they have to do is walk about the stage without crashing into the furniture, face the audience, and shout out stuff that someone else had the intelligence to write.

FRINGE THEATRE

Is better than West End theatre because inevitably you know someone in the cast, which is why you get a free ticket to sit in a room above a pub watching your mate do something he will regret for life. The reason why fringe theatre is better than West End, is that you can take your pint in with you and sit close enough to the set to be able to nick things. That's how I got a samovar, anyway.

SHAKESPEARE

Whenever I see any Shakespeare – let's say I've been kidnapped from the pub – I always make a huge effort to laugh very loudly at the clowns because I know how it feels to be on stage with rubbish material, wishing you were dead. So I try to be encouraging with my peals of merry mirth, which unfortunately makes me sound as though I've just got out of a secure unit, and it tends to make the actor paranoid.

I find it quite difficult to forgive Shakespeare, especially considering that I once got so bored during *A Winter's Tale* that I did a massive yawn, dislocated my jaw and had to wear a metal brace. The only thing that puts Shakespeare up in my estimation is that he got away with writing so much rubbish *and* shagged his sister.

IN SUPERMARKETS

I go with the intention of getting a dodgy trolley and seeing how much ankle skin I can collect around the wheels. Did you ever wonder what that jar of olives is doing in the middle of the sanitary - products? That's my attempt at conceptual art.

I always look out for promotional freebies in supermarkets. Now and again your local will go all French, which means a failed model hovering about, offering you teeny bits of Ardenne paté on soggy toast and plastic thimbles of Côte du Rhone. After a few hundred circuits around the shop floor, you're very, very drunk indeed. If you're sick before you get outside, blame it on the paté.

Let me tell you a true story about something that once happened to me in a supermarket: I was shopping with my daughter, who, at the time, was a toddler. You know what a nightmare they are, always demanding your attention and no matter how many times you smack them, they're always there pulling at your sleeve, so anyway, I'm in this supermarket and I'm reaching up for something from the top shelf. I'm on my tip toes and all I could feel was this tug, tug, tugging, at my tampon string. I wouldn't have minded but it wasn't even my daughter, it was this spotty seventeen-year-old shelf-stacker, who was trying to alert me to the fact that I was standing on his other hand.

CORNER SHOPS IN NORFOLK

These are crap because they do not sell things like fennel or pine kernels, not that I use fennel or pine kernels, it's just good to go into some potato head's shop and demand these things so that they feel inferior, because the only thing they sell is lard. I remember going into a corner shop somewhere in the sticks and asking for a packet of super Lil-lets. What he actually gave me was a packet of lentil soup, whereupon I turned to him and said, 'Oh, very tasty, but it's not going to stem the flow of blood that is issuing forth from my vagina, is it? At which point he was sick, fainted, and I was able to help myself to the contents of his till, although this was a pointless exercise as because they are so backward in the country it was full of threepenny bits.

IN COMMUNAL DRESSING ROOMS

These are the only places where the mirrors are adequately positioned for you to inspect your genitalia under a good strong light. This will traumatise any fifteen-year-old who happens to wander in and catch you with your wrinkly haunches artfully displayed. Remind these girls that what you are looking at is their future.

DIY SHOP

See if you arouse suspicion by asking for an axe, some rope, a spade, and enough wood to make a coffin-shaped box.

MARKS & SPENCER

It is rare for branches of M&S to have changing rooms, but don't let this stop you trying on bras on the shop floor. People visit M&S to buy things like baked potatoes and grated cheese, because you can't make those by yourself. Bake a potato? How? Grate cheese? You mean, use a cheese grater? Oh no, very dangerous, leave it to the experts because you never know when your hand is going to slip and take the skin off your clitoris. At the bottom of some of M&S's sandwich packs you get a funny perforated gusset thing which may be doubled up as a pant liner – definitely a bonus.

SURPRISE PARTIES

These always have disastrous consequences, as we will have seen in many a sit com. The general plot has a girl coming in after a hard day at work. She is tired and does not switch the lights on, unaware that thirty of her closest friends are hiding in various places. Before the arrival of her husband, who is, in fact, hiding under the rug, she calls her lover, slags off all her mates and her spouse, and engages in a lot of smutty talk before switching the light on to reveal the appalled faces of her nearest and dearest. The scene always ends on the mournful note of a curly trumpet thing being blown really half-heartedly.

SHOWBIZ PARTIES

To be quite honest, if I go to a party these days and it's full of old friends, none of whom are famous, so I tend to get really bored and leave early. Parties are only any good if lots of famous people are there. When I go to showbiz parties (which I do), I like to be over-friendly with Jonathan Ross because he's about the only famous person I've ever met who is too kind to tell you to just fuck off. Unfortunately, his wife isn't. Still, it wasn't much of a fight, what with her being pregnant I won easily. I also take the precaution of inserting a battery-operated flashbulb behind my ear, which I can trigger to go off every three seconds. This means people gravitate towards me in the hope of getting into *Hello*. The disadvantage is that you find yourself surrounded by members of the *Eastenders* cast. Body language is all important at celeb bashes, so make sure you're wearing something that your bottom falls out of. Also, never look anyone in the eye while you're talking to them. The correct eyeline is just over the shoulder, so you can see if anyone more famous walks in. I mean, you don't want to be stuck with Christopher Biggins when Robert De Niro makes an entrance.

DINNER PARTIES

I do not like giving dinner parties. This is because I can't cook and I get very nervous. So I start drinking. This is why I have a hostess trolley; I need it to wheel myself in on. The good thing about dinner parties is that you can sit down throughout. This is great because you can get really pissed and no one realises until you wet yourself rather than try and walk to the toilet. Whenever I have a dinner party I invite six people because that's how many plates I've got.

Over the years I have learned not to be too ambitious in what I serve. I usually opt for pasta with that pesto sauce which comes in a handy jar from a supermarket near you (unless you live in Norfolk, where they only sell lard).

Parties

Usually, the combination of pasta and pesto is very tasty, but not, however, when you mistake that old jar of jam that's 98 per cent mould for the pesto. A lot of my friends ended up with bacterial infections.

When couples go to dinner parties together, they always arrive on the doorstep having just had a humdinger of a row. This adds to the air of tension around a table, where for some reason, the hostess has decided to invite a selection of people who do not know each other and have nothing in common. Eating in strained circumstances really aggravates irritable bowel syndrome. All the guests have to go home early before they relax their stomach muscles and a wild fart emerges. I remember my sister's husband telling her that he was leaving her a few minutes before six of his clients turned up for supper. In between courses he went upstairs and packed. She retained her composure right until the end, when she went upstairs and scraped the left overs of the meal into his suitcases.

The most badly behaved dinner-party guests are the ones who forget to tell their host that they are fructarians. In fact, they only eat things that fall naturally to the ground. These are the type of people that bring their own conkers and nibble them in a martyred kind of a way. When I was younger, I went through a bulimic stage (anything for attention). With bulimia you feel compelled to throw up everything you've just eaten. It's a very anti-social disease, especially if you don't bother to leave the table before you yip. But it's one way of putting the candles out at dinner parties, I can tell you. Anorexics make the ideal dinner party guests because they don't eat anything. They pretend to, but you'll find they've hidden everything except the parsley garnish in their napkin. This is great because you can salvage it and eat it for lunch the next day. Great big, fat, greedy people on the other hand, are a nightmare because they eat so much. Mind you, most of them are a bit embarrassed at being so greedy, that they offer to do the washing up. This they do really slowly in between eating bits of leftover fatty bits, making secret lemon-curd sandwiches and rifling through the After Eight packets to see if one's been missed.

Bad table manners are very funny. The ability to cut a piece of meat so that it bounces off your knife and into someone's cleavage is an admirable skill. Score five extra points for digging it out yourself.

Be self-opinionated, insist on ramming your political and religious points of view down everyone's' throats. Turn into Ian Paisley over the cheese board. They will turn up the Dire Straits and try and drown you out, so always take a battery-operated megaphone with you. I don't know about you, but whenever I go to other people's houses to eat, the first thing I do is visit their bathroom. Once I've safely locked the door, I rifle through their medicine cabinets. At least then I'm forewarned about what I could catch if they've been preparing the food without bothering to wash their hands. I also steal toilet rolls because I was once a student and I can't get out of the habit. I also don't really have an excuse for stealing that Yves St Laurent lipstick that is just sitting there saying, 'Take me, take me.'

BARBECUE PARTIES

These are the ideal solution if you can't cook. The only problem with the first barbecue of the season is remembering where you chucked it at the end of

spent all night offering this slop around saying, 'Do have some ratatouille, just try and pick out as much cat shit as you can.'

HOUSE PARTIES

Not as popular these days, because all the rich people who used to invite hordes of people for the weekend have squandered all their money on drug rehabilitation and now spend their weekends wandering round council estates in Hackney trying to score drugs. Still, there are the odd few left who have more money than sense and invite you up to their castle in Scotland which, if they had a brain, they'd swap for a studio flat in the Docklands. Obviously it's very crap to be impressed by a big, turreted house with loads of bedrooms and servants. Make sure you demonstrate your scorn by drawing on the walls and cutting small holes in their curtains. Remember not to take anything like booze or chocs with you, arrive with a huge dog turd on your shoe, a bin liner full of soiled clothing and a broken bunch of carnations from a petrol station. Embark upon your own private class war and tell them their house is very cold. Borrow heaps of cashmere sweaters and 'accidentally' forget to return them. Insist that this weekend should be done properly, like an Evelyn Waugh book. When they ask what you'd like for breakfast, tell them, proper Scottish oats with hot milk and a little honey, smoked kippers, bacon and kidneys, scrambled eggs and croissants, preferably with homemade gooseberry and ginger preserve. Demand a gun so that you can go out hunting, shooting and fishing. Come back at lunchtime having killed the family dog and the contents of the ornamental lake, chuck a few bullet-riddled Japanese Koi on the kitchen table and insist that they should be fried up for lunch and that the peacock which you strangled on the lawn would

last summer, digging it out of the bottom of the garden and scraping the rust off it. You can cook more or less anything on a barbecue because by the time it's all ready it will be dark and people will be too pissed to notice what they're eating. This is my excuse for patiently chewing on an oven glove for a long time, anyway. Barbecued food is either very burnt or very raw. The only way to make sure your chicken leg is done according to how you like it, is to sneak it into the microwave. Another advantage of barbecues is that if you make a very strong marinade, you can use it to disguise the fact that you have bought very cheap meat which the butcher was just about to chuck out. A mixture of turps and marmite gives rancid meat that little piquancy. Listen to me, I haven't got a clue what I'm talking about, I don't cook! Although, I remember reading a recipe book by a famous cookery lady who has a very novel way with ratatouille. What she does is slice her aubergines, courgettes, onions and mushrooms, arranges them in a large earthenware bowl, which she then places on the backstep of her farmhouse in Provence, 'to cook in the sun'. Last time I was having a barbecue I thought that would be nice, so I tried it. The only thing is, I live in Camberwell. I

make a tasty casserole for supper. It is easy to be house guest from hell, just behave naturally. When they say, 'make yourself at home', take it literally. Leave toenail clippings on the Chinese carpet, redecorate your guest bedroom, tell them those frescoes were really getting you down, replenish your supply of logs by carving up the four poster, have wild and noisy sex by yourself, use their telephone to tell your friends how bored you are, sniff their cutlery and ask if they'd mind washing it properly as it smells of dog sick, flick ash into their Ming vase, accuse their old family retainer of feeling you up, and before you go, remove the batteries from their radios, shavers and remote controls. As you leave, tell them that as you've enjoyed it so much, you've recommended it to your mother and she's coming next weekend with her friend Mavis – the one in the wheelchair – so they'd better hurry up and organise some ramps.

OFFICE CHRISTMAS PARTIES

These are most successful if you work in an office, or at least somewhere other people go every day. Sadly I work at home by myself, so my office Xmas parties tend to be a rather sorry affair. At least I make the effort. I start by sending myself an invitation at the beginning of November, requesting the pleasure of my own company the Wednesday before Christmas Day. From then on I tend to get a over excited, culminating in having a very bad perm. This is why I always end up at my office Christmas party wearing a turban. I also make the same mistake every year of buying myself a party dress which does nothing for me. Yet come the day, I put the dress, a new pair of tights and a pair of high-heeled shoes in a plastic bag so that I can change at lunch time.

On the day of the party, I find it quite hard to concentrate. I'm forever looking at my watch, hoping that it's time to go to the ladies' (my bathroom) and glam up. Finally 12.30 arrives, and with much girlish laughter I rush off to transform myself into something rather irresistible. I then spend the next couple of hours making small talk, drinking sweet white wine and eating twiglets all by myself. In true office Christmas-party tradition, I buy a load of sausage rolls which I tread into the carpet, cover myself with that spray-can silly string which I pretend amuses me, when it fact it makes me furious, and end up touching myself up under my desk, while Slade sing '*So here it is Merry Christmas*' for the umpteenth time. At about 3pm , having realised that it's a waste of time going back to 'work', I take myself outside and conga around the block. Obviously I am so embarrassed by my behaviour that all the next day I find it impossible to look myself in the eye, which makes shaving very difficult, and I spend the next few days with bits of bloodied toilet paper on my chin.

Other people's office Christmas parties are a constant source of irritation. I get really fed up of spending the entire month of December standing on the platform of the Northern Line as train after train whistles by without stopping, due to the fact that so many office girls have thrown up on their way home that they are, and I quote the excuse given over the tannoy, 'unfit for public use'.

THE TWILIGHT YEARS

BEING OUTRAGEOUS BEFORE IT'S...

TOO LATE!

PENSIONERS are very lucky because they can pretend to have senile dementia and get away with being utterly vile. Even if they have complete control over their bladders, old people must remember to allow urine to trickle out now and again, they are supposed to smell of wee wee. They are also meant to have traces of food down their front which they should insist is dog food, because that's all they can afford.

Commonly in this country, the older you get, the more you start leaning to the right. Which is why a lot of old people walk funny. There's nothing physically wrong with them, they are just literally walking Fascists. Becoming a raving Tory Bigot is more fun than having an allotment. Even if you've been a fully paid up member of the Socialist Workers party all your life it is the elderly persons prerogative to suddenly switch sides and start slagging off Foreigners and single parents. This is even more effective if you're black and have single handedly brought up six kids. Actually, people will think that you're being ironic and within no time you'll have your own comedy series on Channel 4.

People have a lot of preconceived ideas about what old people should be like. Little children expect Grannies to have cheeks like apples, knit jumpers and bake cakes. They expect Grandpas to make models and mend things. Make sure if you are a grandparent that you are incapable of doing any of this because you're too pissed. It is a good idea to make your Grandchildren too frightened of you

THINGS YOU CAN GET AWAY WITH WHEN YOU'RE ELDERLY

HITTING COPPERS, accusing your chiropodist of sexual molestation, lunging at female members of the Royal Family (only not Anne because she's sexually unattractive), growing beards (women only), and accidentally French kissing your dishy Grandson on his 21st in front of all his friends.

to ever want to come and stay, Grandchildren are a waste of time until they are old enough to be sent round the corner to fetch your fags.

PEOPLE WHO BEHAVE BADLY AS A RESULT OF HAVING WON THE POOLS.

…THERE YOU ARE, STRUGGLING along without a fitted kitchen, kids hate you because you can't afford to buy them a decent pair of trainers, the car's making a funny noise and you're down to your last 10p for the leccy. Then what happens? The people next door win the pools. Life's a bitch, the wrong people are always winning the pools, particularly those that actually do them. I'd use the money to piss everyone off and never draw a sober breath, it would be pink champagne and Cadillacs all the way. Would I forget my friends? Too right, they couldn't afford to keep up. And anyway, you know how difficult it is to find a babysitter. I'd have new friends— rich ones that know all the groovy places to eat and drink; friends that wear nice clothes and go abroad.

I JUST WOULDN'T HAVE anything in common with my old friends, it would be pointless to try and keep in touch. Immediately after having won, I'd probably send them a fax saying something like, 'nice to have known you'. Not that any of them have fax machines, so they wouldn't get it—there you go, it's easy to lose touch! They'd probably come round to my house ligging on my good fortune, hoping to get a teaspoon of caviar, pretending they don't care how much money I've got; it's me they like and, by the way, can they borrow a tenner 'til they get their giro? Well they can try, but I won't be in because I'll have moved, somewhere that's got big iron gates and a real live Game Show Host living next door. If they try and phone me, I'll get the maid to say I'm having supper down the road with Cilla and Bobby. Of course it would be nice to be able to help out my old mum and dad, but sod it, they didn't give me stuff I wanted when I was a kid in case I turned into a spoilt brat. Well, now the boot is on the other foot. Yes, an orthopaedic bed would be nice, but we don't want you getting spoilt now, do we parents dear?

Because I am very shit with money, if I won the Pools, I would take very bad advice from dodgy finance companies and do daft things like open up a silk worm farm in Norfolk. I'd export beetroot to Latvia, singlehandedly support a West End Musical based on the life story of Bouncer, the dog from neighbours, buy a load of Government Bonds and wait for it to all go down the toilet. During this time, as every branch of my eating joints for Bulimics (The Vomitariums) go to the wall and I'm forced to eat humble pie (which is about the only thing you can't get from Harrods Food Hall), then I shall write a screen play about my life, sell it to Francis Ford Coppola, let his niece play me, and move to Hollywood where they know how to treat millionaires properly.

Jenny Eclair's Book Of Bad Behaviour

RULES FOR PEOPLE WHO HAVE JUST WON THE POOLS

DO NOT ATTEMPT TO KEEP IT UNDER YOUR MATTRESS, YOU'LL NEVER GET A DECENT NIGHTS KIP— And anyway, you may possibly wet the bed what with the excitement of having met Bob Holness at the presentation, in which case it will turn into papier mache—which is not legal tender.

IGNORE ALL BEGGING LETTERS— They only want your money so that their children can walk again.

TAKE UP SMOKING —You can afford to now, and if you get cancer at least you'll be able to buy a really expensive wig.

PUT A RED HANDKERCHIEF IN THE WASHING MACHINE WITH ALL YOUR WHITE SHIRTS—Who cares if the hanky runs and everything goes pink, you can go out and get some new white shirts.

HAVE A NEW SET OF CONTACT LENSES EVERYDAY—George Michael does, and you're richer than he is, not that you wear contact lenses, but that's not the point

BUY A TIMESHARE—Because its the easiest way of wasting money that you can think of. Ditto racehorses.

OFFER YOUR BROTHER IN LAW THE NISSAN CHERRY—He can have it for £1,500.

SEND THE WIFE ON A CRUISE—Make sure you've changed the locks by the time she gets back. Just because you've been married for thirty years doesn't entitle her to a share of the pickings. There's tarts out there, you may have a goiter, but fuck it, you're a millionaire!

GET A BIDET —You don't know what they're for, but the dog likes them.

Go into car showrooms and say, ' I'll have that in gold, pink and puce'. Because you can.

£40.04   14 X's

£85.80   15 X's

EQUIPMENT FOR OLD PEOPLE, C

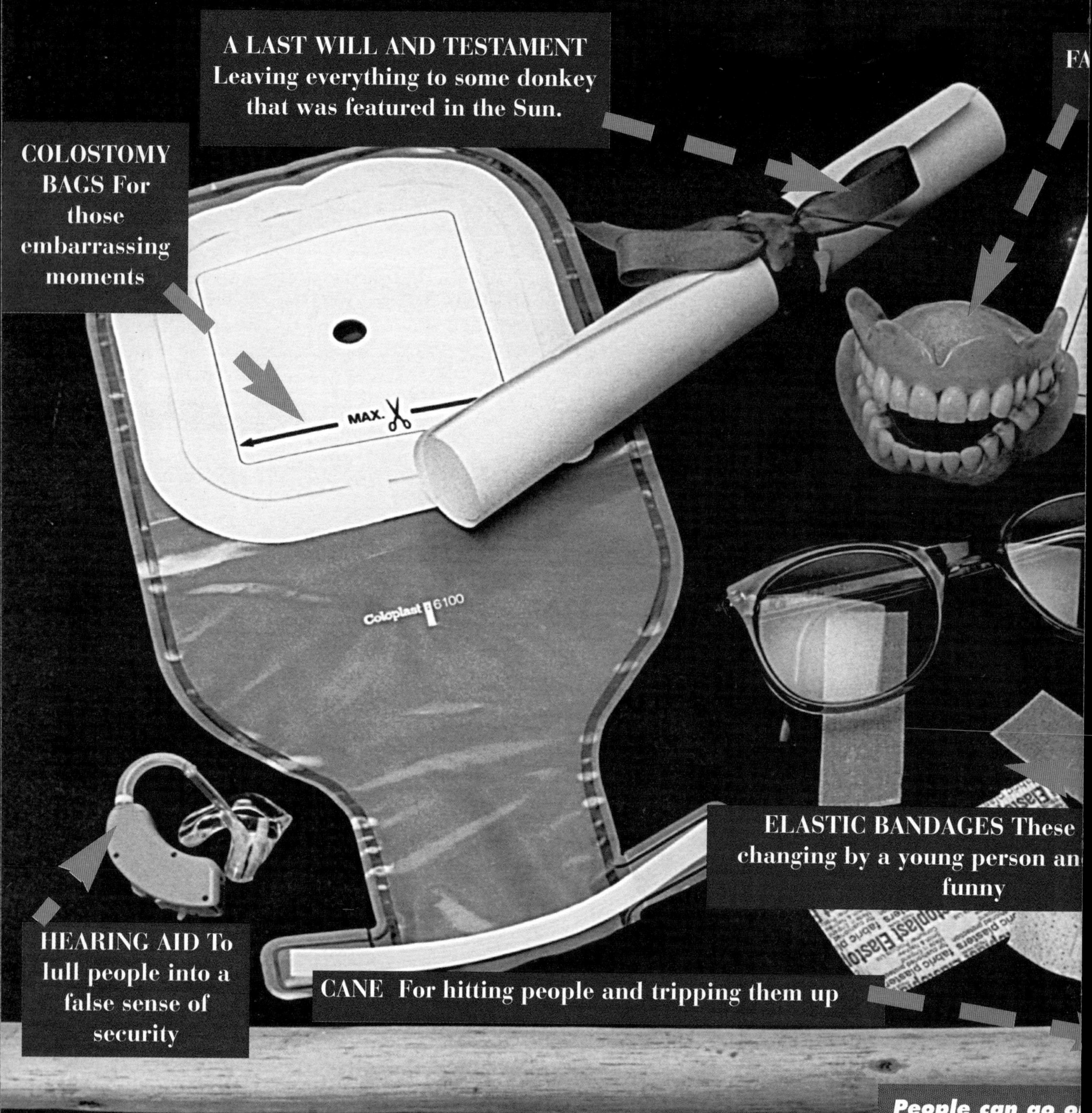

People can go o
a myth that 'You
buried along wit

DRIVING LICENCE You may be half blind but that's not going to stop you going out on the road and driving at three miles an hour

Old people love to travel. At peak times, Victoria Coach Station is full of little old ladies with grey hair and determined jaws, swarming on and off coaches. They don't care where they're going just as long as they get the seat next to the driver who they try and tempt into a sexual liaison with butterscotch. I was once instructed by my boyfriend to pick his mother up from Victoria Coach Station. It was Christmas Eve, the place was hopping with little old frails with bandages round their ankles, and they all looked exactly the same; very little and wrinkly, eyes shining with malice. I picked up the nearest one and bundled her into the back of the car. Half an hour later, she was still jabbering on in Welsh I realised my mistake. I kept quiet, and it was the best Christmas in years. In fact, we became quite close, and when she died (on Boxing Day) I was almost sad.

THE WONDERFUL thing about the advancement of modern medicine is that people are able to wear shell suits longer. These days the streets are full of ancient people in turquoise nylon, leaping onto coaches on their way to Spain, their sole motive being to spend your inheritance. I think a lot of them are on drugs, certainly the saga trips to Amsterdam are very popular, but that's the old of today for you. Time was when geriatrics had a tipple of Warninks at Xmas and that was their lot (apart from my nan, who used to get off on the brine left in a jar of pickled gherkins). These days it's all Malibu and letters to Womans Realm from 70 year old women who think they might have contracted V.D.

Drawing your pension is licence to misbehave. People are terrified of telling you off in case you have the vapours and keel over. Exploit this if you're an old lady, accidentally on purpose forget to put your drawers on, then sit around with your legs open creating a mighty

n utter nightmare, even when they're dead. It is
ke it with you". Yes you can, insist that you are
g of value that you ever possessed.

95

draught. Old men should make a point of 'forgetting' to do their flies up and letting their willy show a lot.

LISTEN, THESE PEOPLE fought a war for us, they've got a right to expose their genitalia. What they haven't got a right to do is give you a measly shilling for your birthday, the tight arsed gits. Actually that's the problem with most old people; their arses aren't tight enough and whiffy smells trump out constantly.

The ultimate way for an old person to embarrass their family is to appear on 'Coffin Dodgers Blind Date'. They just can't resist making lots of lewd remarks about how they may be old, but they're gagging for it. The studio audience loves them, but their grandchildren are so humiliated that going to school becomes a trauma and they have to be privately tutored at home.

Old people can cause utter havoc by suddenly becoming too feeble to look after themselves, so unless you can fork out for one of those nursing homes that will neglect them to death, they have to move in with you. At this point the old gimmer in question will perk up and live for another twenty years playing spin the bottle with the couple next door.

FUNERALS

NORMALLY VERY sad occasions, unless of course you have just been widowed by a very fat rich man, in which case it's a good idea to wear one of those hats with a veil so that people can't see you grinning. Cremation seems to be more popular these days than the old fashioned box in the ground method, though most films still favour the lowering of the coffin into freshly dug earth, because it has more poignancy. Standing on the side of a grave can be fraught with danger however. A rather plump girlfriend of mine was in the process of throwing a single rose onto the coffin of a recently departed relative, when she lost her balance and toppled into the grave. As people stepped forward to help, the edges of the graveside caved in and several of them fell in. It was all rather undignified but none the less, extremely funny.

Because I live in a rather tough part of South East London, I see a lot of funeral processions for local villains. There's always loads of hearses smothered in floral tributes made up in the shape of crow bars and safes and pints of beer. These are followed by umpteen Jags stuffed full of people who have popped over from Malaga to pay their respects. For some reason I often get stuck in the middle of theses processions in my Fiat Panda. But that's nowhere near as bad as the bunch of carnival floats with people dressed up as the cast of 'Allo,Allo', caught up in a very sombre funeral cortege on the Walworth Rd.

Many old folk with nothing better to do than scour through the local papers to check that they themselves haven't passed away, will opt to attend a funeral rather than a jumble sale. All they need is a hat and a hankie and they will find themselves whisked away after the service in cousin Norm's Sierra to the deceased's house for Sherry and fruit cake. It's best to do your homework first, it's no good standing around saying things like, 'He was such a kind, gentle man', if the dead man died in a stabbing incident in a pub down the Old Kent Rd.

Cremations are not devoid of comic potential, especially when the urn gets dropped and the ashes scatter. This is what happened to SidVicious, whose mum dropped his urn at Heathrow Airport having gone all the way to the States to get it. The ashes were sucked up into an air vent, and to this day, Sid's ashes continue to circle around the air conditioning system. Which is probably why the food tastes like it does at Heathrow.

So remember, even dead, we can all behave badly. Good luck!